The
ELECTRIFIED
TEEN

Unleashing God's Design in Christian Youth

Jacob E. Wilcox

WESTBOW
PRESS®
A DIVISION OF THOMAS NELSON
& ZONDERVAN

Scripture taken from the New King James Version®. Copyright © 1982 by
Thomas Nelson. Used by permission. All rights reserved.

Scriptures taken from the Holy Bible, New International Version®, NIV®. Copyright © 1973,
1978, 1984, 2011 by Biblica, Inc.™ Used by permission of Zondervan. All rights reserved
worldwide. www.zondervan.com The "NIV" and "New International Version" are trademarks
registered in the United States Patent and Trademark Office by Biblica, Inc.™

Scripture quotations taken from the New American Standard Bible® (NASB),
Copyright © 1960, 1962, 1963, 1968, 1971, 1972, 1973,
1975, 1977, 1995 by The Lockman Foundation
Used by permission. www.Lockman.org

Scripture quotations marked (NLT) are taken from the Holy Bible, New Living Translation,
copyright ©1996, 2004, 2007, 2013, 2015 by Tyndale House Foundation. Used by permission
of Tyndale House Publishers, Inc., Carol Stream, Illinois 60188. All rights reserved.

Scripture quotations marked (NIrV) are taken from the Holy Bible, New International Reader's Version®,
NIrV® Copyright © 1995, 1996, 1998, 2014 by Biblica, Inc.™ Used by permission of Zondervan. All
rights reserved worldwide. www.zondervan.com The "NIrV" and "New International Reader's Version"
are trademarks registered in the United States Patent and Trademark Office by Biblica, Inc.™

WestBow Press books may be ordered through booksellers or by contacting:

WestBow Press
A Division of Thomas Nelson & Zondervan
1663 Liberty Drive
Bloomington, IN 47403
www.westbowpress.com
1 (866) 928-1240

Because of the dynamic nature of the Internet, any web addresses or links contained in
this book may have changed since publication and may no longer be valid. The views
expressed in this work are solely those of the author and do not necessarily reflect the views
of the publisher, and the publisher hereby disclaims any responsibility for them.

Any people depicted in stock imagery provided by Thinkstock are models,
and such images are being used for illustrative purposes only.
Certain stock imagery © Thinkstock.

ISBN: 978-1-9736-1660-3 (sc)
ISBN: 978-1-9736-1662-7 (hc)
ISBN: 978-1-9736-1661-0 (e)

Library of Congress Control Number: 2018901025

Print information available on the last page.

WestBow Press rev. date: 01/29/2018

This book is dedicated to my family and friends in faith. Stay strong my friends, have faith, and keep fighting the good fight; the Godly fight.

"Don't let anyone look down on you because you are young, but set an example for the believers in speech, in love, in faith, and in purity."
– 1 Timothy 4:12 NIV

Contents

Introduction

Some say Teenagers are the church of the future, but I say we are the church of today, and leaders of tomorrow. There are very few active teenagers in church today; why is this? It is because we have failed to focus on, and address situations that teenagers go through on a daily basis: Temptation, peer pressure, depression, Self harm, Bullying, and others. Since we have failed to address these situations biblically, before they took root into their lives, they've walked away from the faith and church thinking that the church and its occupants are all haters and intolerant fools.

When they departed from our Christian culture, they also departed from good morals and just reasoning; they lost all respect for adults; so what can we do as teenagers? We must take over those positions of leadership and spiritually electrify our generation into the Faith. To do this you need to know how to properly address the situations in their lives. Using scripture and biblical knowledge which is found in this book you can accomplish this task. So go fellow Teenager and young adults; go and electrify your community for the Christian faith.

Opening Words

Hello! My name is Jacob Wilcox. Some like to call me Jake but, I would love if you just call me Jacob. I just wanted to talk for a minute about this book, who I am, why I am writing such a book, and how you should read this book.

Let's start with me and my journey to get to where I am now: I am 16 years old; that's right a teenager writing a book! That probably sounds strange to you, but it's true. Don't let my age fool you though; I am like a box crammed fool of any and every kind of knowledge I can get my hands on. But, being an introvert makes it kind of difficult to release any such knowledge to the world verbally (that's another reason why I'm writing this book).

I'm also a homeschool student. I've been homeschooled my entire life. I've only stepped into a public school once and that was just a couple of feet inside the door. You might say I'm average; although I've heard from a non-Christian that "I am a different breed of human" because of how I live in my faith.

When it comes to situations that almost every teen and young adult goes through I am no different.

Some people would say "oh you're a Christian homeschooler, you don't go through the same stuff we do at 'normal' school." Trust me just because someone is homeschooled doesn't mean that their life is totally separated from 21st century situations. I remember one time I heard someone say: "Why don't you go to real school?" Homeschooling is as real as it gets, but I won't get into a debate on which one is better.

OK, let's talk about why I started this book, shall we? I started this book because I felt like there is little known about young adults. Many people simply don't understand youth let alone their situations and problems they face daily. (Sometimes youth don't even understand how to deal with situations that they approach). So I set out to reveal the mysteries of a teenager's situations. I want youth of every age to know that there is a person who understands them, and wants to help them. After all I am a teenager myself. I should get some credit for that.

My goal is to raise an army of strong, fearless, faithful, and righteous teenage believers who:

Can stand strong in the faith
And defend their own kingdom (their mind).

Teenagers, when faced with troublesome situations, can conquer and use those situations as a foothold – if shown how.

Just like the castles and realms of old, I want to knight you. I want you to become a Christian knight. But, to be a knight one must have armor, and what's better than God's armor that He gives us? *"Finally, be strong in the Lord and in his mighty power. Put on the full armor of God so that you can take your stand against the devil's schemes. For our struggle is not against flesh and blood, but against the rulers, against the authorities, against the powers of this dark world and against the spiritual forces of evil in the heavenly realms. Therefore put on the full armor of God, so that when the day of evil comes, you may be able to stand your ground... Stand firm then, with the belt of truth buckled around your waist, with the breastplate of righteousness in place, and with your feet fitted with the readiness that comes from the gospel of peace. In addition to all this, take up the shield of faith, with which you can extinguish all the flaming arrows of the evil one. Take the helmet of salvation and the sword of the Spirit, which is the word of God." – Ephesians 6:10-1 NIV.*

Hopefully by the end of this book, you will be inspired to go train and teach others what you have learned. That's our mission, to spiritually electrify our friends, our youth group, and others; but it starts with you. If you want change in your school, country, city, family, etc., then you must first change yourself, and change others.

Read this book with the intention of being changed by it. If you read this book with no intention of gaining knowledge, you will not gain anything.

So let's start your quest of becoming an Electrified teen.

Part one

CONDUCTING A CHRISTIAN LIFE

One

The Basics of Christianity

*Don't let anyone look down on you because you
are young, but set an example for the believers in
speech, in life, in love, in faith and in purity.*
f– 1 Timothy 4:12 NIV

You are the light of the world, a city on a hill.
– Matthew 5:14 NIV

As Christian teens we're faced with a lot of ridicule and peer pressure. We get bullied for not doing what the world does. Sometimes we try to fit in with the world....but think of it this way, did Jesus ever try to fit in? No. He stood out among the people. One major reason He stood out among the believers was that He loved sinners. Many Jews of His day didn't associate with Gentiles, yet He did.

> *You are all sons of the light and sons of the day. We do not belong to the night or to the darkness.*
> *1 Thessalonians 5:5 NIV*

This is sad today because a lot of churches have drawn this fine line between Christians and Non-Christians. If you're on the other side of this line, they will start to judge you and think that you're not as good as them. We as Christians need to get rid of that line and love like Jesus did.

There is a great deal of older folks out there that have no hope for us youth today. Some think we're just a lost cause, therefore they tend to look at us like we're unimportant, but we are very important! Not only are we the future of the church but we are also the church of right now.

A big problem with churches that have youth and adults in the same setting is the worship: <u>their way of worship is different from the way we worship</u>. I have come across some people that think the only way we can worship God is through the old hymns. But don't get me wrong, the old hymns are still valuable in worship. The problem is that those certain people think those are the only type of music you can sing to praise God.

I long for a day where young and old alike can come together and worship without all the bickering about certain songs. It's not about which songs are better, it's about glorifying Jesus. So as long as the song glorifies Jesus then you're okay!

> We are spiritual warriors for Christ.

You need to understand that "older" people like "older" music; we all like different styles of music. That's not bad. All Christian songs are pretty much the same, they all are glorifying God (or at least should be). What's bad is when a person who doesn't like the particular kind of music that he/she is hearing, starts thinking selfishly and strays away from what the song's original purpose is for: glorifying God.

<u>Worship however you want, whether it is with lifted hands or silent lips</u>.

"For I am not ashamed of the gospel of Christ: for it is the power of God unto salvation to everyone that believeth... – Romans 1:16 KJV.

One very important statement is that Christians are not perfect. We go to church and seek Jesus because we are broken and messed up (at least that's what we are suppose to do). The only way to put us back together is through divine intervention. Christians stumble and fall but by the grace of God we can just get back up and fight even harder.

Questions

1. What are some ways you worship?
2. What are some ways we can set examples for other believers?
3. How did Jesus stand out among people?

Two

My Message to You

*Don't let the excitement of youth cause you to forget your Creator.
Honor him in your youth before you grow old and say, "Life is
not pleasant anymore." Remember him before the light of the
sun, moon, and stars is dim to your old eyes, and rain clouds
continually darken your sky. Remember him before your legs-the
guards of your house-start to tremble; and before your shoulders-
the strong men-stoop. Remember him before your teeth — your
few remaining servants — stop grinding; and before your eyes —
the women looking through the windows — see dimly. —
Ecclesiastes 12:1-3 NIV*

*Rebellion is as bad as the sin of witchcraft, and stubbornness
is as bad as worshipping idols. — 1 Samuel 15:23a NLT*

*Never speak harshly to an older man, but appeal to him
respectfully as though he were your own father. Talk to
the younger men as you would to your own brothers. Treat
older women as you would your mother, and treat younger
women with all purity as you would your own sister.
— 1 Timothy 5:1-2 NLT*

*Fear not, for I am with you; Be not dismayed, for I am your
God. I will strengthen you, yes, I will help you, I will uphold
you with my righteous right hand. — Isaiah 41:10 NKJV*

"**Y**our age doesn't define your maturity, your grades don't define your intellect, and rumors don't define who you are." – Author Unknown.

As Christian teenagers we must minister to other teenagers. A great deal of youth out there will ignore pastors or adults, because they simply think that religion is an adult thing, and that they're just trying to tell them "what to do." So we need to step up and show them that it isn't. We as Christian youth need to tell other youth about Jesus. Teens will listen to other teens. Get the word out to the youth and invite them to church, and love them like Christ loves us.

> Christianity is more than coming to Church and fulfilling your Church "to do" list.

As Christian teenagers, we are the light for other teens and adults. So go and bring teens onto the right path and encourage them to make right choices. One thing you can't do is force them; they have their own free will, so just encourage the good stuff they do and discourage the wrong stuff. But be careful for they will try to bring you into their lifestyle.

Most of all you must be patient; they're not going to become a Christian overnight. It takes time. It might take years, months, or minutes. Just be patient, pray, and have faith.

> We do not draw people to Christ by loudly discrediting what they believe, by telling them how wrong they are and how right we are, but by showing them a light that is so lovely that they want with all their hearts to know the source of it.
> – Madeleine L' Engle

Standing out

As Christians we are to stand out among other teens; one way of doing this is by respecting your elders. Who are your elders? They are anybody who is older then you (parents, grandparents, cops, neighbors…). If you start respecting them they'll start to respect you.

"How good and pleasant it is when brothers live together in unity." – *Psalms 133:1 NIV.*

Another way of standing out is not doing what the world does; you need to not take part in your friend's wrong doings. Let's say you had a friend named Jim. One day Jim invited you to a party were there will be drinking and other sinful activities. Even if you are not going to participate in any of that you shouldn't even consider going. If Jim asks why, then that would be a good time to tell him about your faith and witness to him.

I say "if the world does something do the complete opposite." *"Let us behave properly as in the day, not in carousing and drunkenness, not in sexual promiscuity and sensuality, not in strife and jealousy. But put on the Lord Jesus Christ, and make no provision for the flesh in regard to its lusts."* – *Romans 13:1-14 NASB.*

Stay away from that person when they try to tempt you, don't participate in their wrong doings. *"My son if sinners entice you, do not give in to them."* – *Proverbs 1:10 NIV.*

Never give up fighting for them, God is always with you to strengthen your body and your faith.

"He gives strength to the weary and increases the power of the weak. Even youths grow tired and weary, and young men stumble and fall; but those who hope in the Lord will renew their strength. They will soar on wings like eagles; they will run and not grow weary, they will walk and not be faint." – *Isaiah 40:29-31 NIV.*

Facing the world

> The way you act when you are alone is who you really are.

Being a Christian means not living like the world does. We are to be in the world but not of it (which I already said). Trust me when I tell you that the world will mock you for being a Christian. If you are not being mocked or shunned then you need to re-examine your Christian life to make sure it's truly all there.

"If the world hates you, you know that it has hated Me before it hated you. If you were of the world, the world would love its own; but because you are not of the world, but I chose you out of the world, because of this the world hates you." – John 15:18-19 NASB.

I just want to make it plain and simple; the world hates us! They want every Christian gone. The world will attack you like a lioness attacking an antelope; they'll do everything they can to make you an illegitimate Christian. I know by experience the details of what people will try to do to us. They trip us, ensnare us, they watch and wait for you to say something that goes against your beliefs.

How do we counter this? We've been on the defensive for so long how do we switch to the offensive? How can we take the battle to the enemy?

The first step is throwing out political correctness. This world is dying to this new trend! We don't have any more time to be politically correct! Say what needs to be said and let life go on! This world has got so tied up in people's feelings.

> "Man's spirit carries his attitude, reactions, and perspectives of life." – Pastor Steve Queen 2016

In life people are going to pick on and mock you. You just have to have some confidence in Christ.

There is a phrase that people have been using lately: "Haters gotta hate." There is so much truth in that phrase. Haters got to hate either you or someone else; just don't get down about what they say. You've got to separate from them, and if possible embrace the positive side of people.

Your attitude and standards should be unique. They shouldn't be what the politically correct crowd says. Being unique is God given. You are you! You are the only you out there. So don't let the world destroy your uniqueness by changing your attitude and standards.

The only person you should be letting mold your standards and attitude upon life is God.

So now that we've got political correctness out of the way, the next step is: Speaking out. When the crowd is actively embracing premarital sex or drugs then speak out against it. Stand your ground even if it means standing alone upon a battlefield surrounded by the worst enemy you can imagine.

Fight for every square inch of the battle zone.

The most productive way of witnessing to the crowd is basically doing nothing. You might not think that at first but, all you need to do is stand there and let the Light of your life shine. People will see that, they'll see how you handle situations that come your way. Remember what I said earlier that they're always watching. You could soften a soul's heart by showing them how you deal with problems that you go through in the right way. If you do it right, the people will know where you stand. They'll know that if something happens in their lives that they can come to you for answers and possibly prayer. But you can only do that if you resist evil and cling to what is just and honorable. The vibe from your very own life will shine on others. It may not look like it at first but you are planting a seed in their life.

So why am I stressing this witnessing thing? It is because people die every single day; many with sin in their hearts. Many are dying as you are reading these very words. Death is a serious thing not to be taken lightly. Life is temporary, death is eternal. If you think suicide is the only option, let me just tell you that it's worse on the other side for someone who commits suicide (which I will address later in this book).

You are going to be dead way longer than you'll be alive. Imagine if you will, the Titanic, one of the biggest ships made. When it sank many of the people died in the icy depths of the ocean. You know what? They are still dead to this day.

When you die there are only two places you can go: Heaven or Hell. If you are going to be dead for eternity why not go somewhere

where you can experience joy, love, kindness, and the direct presence of God?

Live this life for the next.

I've had a certain person come up to me and ask me: "What if there is no afterlife, no Heaven or Hell? And when you die you float around in nothingness?" Here's what I said: If you are right then we have nothing to worry about. A Christian and atheist will die and they'll both float around in nothingness, and life is meaningless.

> *"Turn not to the right nor the left: remove thy foot from evil."–Proverbs 4:27 KJV*

But, if you are wrong and Heaven and Hell do exist, then you, as an atheist, have a lot to worry about. If there is an afterlife then we were created here for a purpose not by an accident. If God exists but did not create a heaven and hell then He is not a holy and righteous God. God is like a father and like a father He punishes His children when they do wrong. If He doesn't punish us then we are not legitimate. Wouldn't you want God to punish someone who broke into your house, murdered your family and stole all your prized possessions? See, God is just in His punishment but since He is so righteous He will also punish liars, people who commit adultery, and even people who wanted to rape, steal, and lie, but never had the chance. God's punishment for their sins is Hell. But God also rewards those who obey and follow Him.

If you are that person who follows God with your whole heart then you have absolutely nothing to worry about; whether you live or die you are His. When you just think about that your whole aspect on life/death will change. I know when I started thinking this way my whole thought process on death changed.

If you just think about it, God's offering us a great gift. When we die we'll be in the direct presence of Him. We will experience the joys of Heaven if we just only believe in our hearts what He did on the cross and confess Him as our Lord and Savior. He's giving us a lot for a little in return. He rewards those who earnestly seek Him.

Death is a long time, so where will you spend it? Death might sound scary but think of it this way: You are not going to die unless God allows it, and if He says so then you can't stop Him. That's my attitude towards death and it has transformed my life for the good.

Lastly we need to show love. Many different social groups hate us because we "hate" them. This world is full of hate, but as the body of Christ we are not to be in the world so why are you "hating?"

"Love the sinner, hate the sin." What's that mean? The person is not the enemy; it's the devil that corrupted them. We are to love and show compassion to the sinners. However there's a difference between loving them and accepting and/or endorsing their evil ways. We are not to compromise. Jesus did not compromise His standards, and He saved millions of souls, so why should we? We must keep in mind that they are still sinners in need of forgiveness. We cannot treat them as any less than us. We are to love and cherish their soul; and try everything we can to witness to them. They're lost and need to be found so guide them on the right path. Spiritually electrify each and every person you encounter; become electrified in Christ.

Three

Discovering God

*The Lord is my light and my salvation; whom shall I fear? The Lord is
the strength of my life; of whom shall I be afraid? – Psalms 27:1 KJV*

*But God is faithful and fair. If we admit that we have sinned,
he will forgive us our sins. He will forgive every wrong thing
we have done. He will make us pure. – 1 John 1:9 NIV*

*Let everyone in the world fear the Lord, and let everyone
stand in awe of Him. For when he spoke, the world began!
It appeared at His command. – Psalms 33:8-9 NLT*

*The Lord looks down from heaven and sees the whole human
race. From his throne he observes all who live on the earth.
– Psalms 33:13-15 NLT*

*For the eyes of the Lord run to and fro throughout the whole earth,
to show himself strong on behalf of those whose heart is loyal to him.
– 2 Chronicles 16:9a KJV*

Some people think God is just like a jolly old guy upstairs or a huge
man in the heavens who is watching you waiting to strike you down
at the moment you do something wrong.

That's not who God is. God is like a loving father. He loves His
children (us) to the point that He even died for us (which I will talk

about later in this book). *"But God commanded his own love toward us, in that, while we were yet sinners, Christ died for us." – Romans 5:8 KJV.*

He is also a forgiving God. He forgives us so many times that if I got a penny for every time He's forgiven me I would be a billionaire. So if He forgives us so many times does that mean we can keep sinning only if we say sorry afterwards? No. God won't forgive sin if you're not truly sorry for it. *"Anyone who hides his sins doesn't succeed. But anyone who admits his sins and gives them up finds mercy." – Proverbs 28:13 NIV.*

Sometimes I hear people say, "God is just up there to punish us, He's the reason why so many disasters are happening." I've also heard that, "When we do something wrong something bad will happen later on." It's true that your decisions might have a negative outcome. For instance, if you have engaged in premarital sex you might end up with an unwanted pregnancy. But it's not God punishing

> God is like a friend that sticks by your side through anything life throws at you.

you. God doesn't "punish" us; He teaches us. God is a teacher, and when we engage in sin He's going to show us the error in our ways. He's going to show us what we did wrong. You might have sinned on a busy day without even knowing it. Your mind is focused on the world so He can't speak to your heart; so what does He need to do? He makes you stop and think in many different ways. He's trying to speak to you but you're just too busy to pay attention.

> God is NOT a genie in a bottle that grants your many wishes; but a person who seeks our friendship.

God's our teacher, our sensei, our master, our commander. What commander doesn't show his soldier what he did wrong? He shows us our errors, and then we must either fix it, or ignore it and carry on with life. Let me tell you, carrying on with life is not a wise decision. I personally have lost a lot of sleep because of my ignorance to heed to His will.

God wants you to humble yourself before Him, and He wants you to turn from your sins and never look back.

"For if we sin willfully after that we have received the knowledge of the truth, there remaineth no more sacrifice for sins, but a certain fearful looking for of judgment and fiery indignation, which shall devour the adversaries." – Hebrews 10:26-27 KJV.

God is also patient (like extremely patient). He's been waiting 6,000 years for us to get right with Him.

He is also a jealous God. He doesn't want you worshipping other God's or other people. He wants you to spend time with Him. If you're spending time with friends then God wants you to spend equal time with Him. He created you so give Him some gratitude, be thankful, and don't worry about the future circumstances because He has it under control. It might look like your life is messed up and confusing but God is leading you through that stuff, if you only stick with Him you will come out victorious.

God wants us to fear Him, but not like a scared and afraid fear but an awe and respectful fear. When you look to God you should fear Him with awe and respect; not cowardice fear but a sense of loving fear.

> "My great concern is not whether God is on our side; my great concern is to be on God's side." – Abraham Lincoln 1809-1865

So who is God to you? Can you describe God and His attitude that you think He has? Here is a quote from a friend, it describes God pretty well. Read it and then make your own description of who you think He is.

"God is my best friend. God is always there for me when I'm happy, sad, angry, or excited. He is my rock; someone that holds me together when I am falling apart.

"He is like a dad that I can talk to about anything and everything as if He is sitting right in front of me.

Jacob E. Wilcox

"God is amazing and powerful.

"Sometimes God gets blamed for letting bad things happen, but in reality He never wants to hurt His children. But when Adam and Eve sinned it allowed hurt into the world. God exists in the world today, even though many people deny and betray Him on a daily basis." – Debra Hill, 2016.

"Endure hardship as discipline; God is treating you as sons. For what son is not disciplined by his father? If you are not disciplined (and everyone undergoes discipline), then you are illegitimate children and not true sons. Moreover, we have all had human fathers who discipline us and we respected them for it. How much more should we submit to the father of our spirits and live! Our fathers disciplined us for a little while as they thought best; but God disciplines us for our good, that we may share in his holiness. No discipline seems pleasant at the time, but painful. Later on, however, it produces a harvest of righteousness and peace for those who have been trained by it. –Hebrews 12:7-11 NIV.

Four

Worldly Prayer

Run from anything that stimulates youthful lust. Follow anything that makes you want to do right. Pursue faith and love and peace, and enjoy the companionship of those who call on the Lord with pure hearts.
—2 Timothy 2:22 NLT

$\mathbf{A}$s Christians we are not to participate in sinful worldly activities like lying, cussing, drinking, drugs, etc. We are to be in the world but not of it. Remember we are just passing through; we are to live for the next life. Many non-Christian people and Christians as well live for this life, like putting all their effort in making money, going to school, etc. That stuff isn't bad, God wants us to get an education so we can provide for our families, but that's not how we are supposed to live. *"It is better to be poor and honest than rich and crooked. —Proverbs 28:6 NLT.*

This life here is just like a blink of an eye compared to eternity after death. I would rather live a life here being bullied, and being poor, and make it into the kingdom of Heaven, than to be rich and popular and not inherit the kingdom of Heaven. And yes I know it's hard not to get wrapped up in worldly things (I

> Obtaining wealth, power, and prestige is what our world strives for but Jesus strives for us to live for Him.

struggle a lot with this also). Just try to keep your focus on God and He will provide. *"The life is more than food and the body is more than clothing."* – *Luke 12:23 NASB.*

We shouldn't spend our life wanting the newest technology or clothes because the body is more than that. *"Many are the plans in a man's heart, but it is the Lord's purpose that prevails."* – *Proverbs 19:21 NIV.*

God created us to worship Him, not worship the material stuff on this Earth; so live for Jesus. Speak to others about Him and if you get ridiculed just remember that God is with you and He cares about you.

Yes it is okay to want or own the latest gadget or newest clothes, but like I said earlier, you can't make that the center of your thinking. Give God the same amount of time as any other important activity. Put God first in all areas of your life. When you're about to make a decision, whether it's important or not, ask God for the right decision.

> What would the world be like if God said yes to every single prayer request you have prayed?

One thing a lot of Christians tend to do (including me sometimes) is put God in a box. They leave Him there while things are going well in life, then when something bad happens they take Him out, and ask for help or forgiveness. Then once the bad thing is gone they shove Him right back in the box. God isn't a genie.

> God waits for you to communicate with Him. You have instant, direct access to God. God loves mankind so much, and in a very special sense His children, that He has made Himself available to you at all times. – Wesley L. Duewel

Think of it this way: how would you treat your closest friend, or how would you want your closest friend to treat you? Would you like it if your best friend only talked to you when he wanted something? We only talk to Him when we want something. We get so selfish sometimes! We think the world revolves around us.

We need to talk to God on the good days and on the bad days.

> God waits for you to communicate with Him. You have instant, direct access to God. God loves mankind so much, and in a very special sense His children, that He has made Himself available to you at all times. – Wesley L. Duewel

So don't just talk to Him before a meal, before you go to sleep, or when you need something. Talk to Him like He's your closest friend. Lack of prayer is a big deal. Your entire relationship with God is based off of prayer. *"Whether you turn to the right or the left, your ears will hear a voice behind you, saying, 'This is the way; walk in it'."* – Isaiah 30:21 NIV.

We need to pray more so God can strengthen us, and help us when we confront secular people. Teens and young adults lose their faith because of lack of prayer; that is just awful. They don't have a firm communication with God so they start to drift away.

"And this is my prayer: that your love may abound more and more in knowledge and depth of insight, so that you may be able to discern what is best and may be pure and blameless until the day of Christ, filled with the fruit of righteousness that comes through Jesus Christ to the glory and praise of God. – Philippians 1:9-11 NIV.

Prayer is very important because it strengthens your friendship with God and it allows God to speak back to you, as long as you're listening to Him. Don't make it a one-way communication. That's not how friendship works. Friendship is a two-way connection in which both parties speak and listen to each other.

> We get so focused and distracted on the issues of life that we forget who the Creator is, and what He can do.

As human beings in this world, we like to be people pleasers. We feel like we need to please every single person out in the world.

You can't do that as a Christian! You have to say that whatever they are doing is wrong. You cannot be a yes-man or woman; sometimes you just have to say no.

"Be very careful, then, how you live – not as unwise but as wise, making the most of every opportunity, because the days are evil. Therefore do not be foolish, but understand what the Lord's will is." – Ephesians 5:15-17 NIV.

"Those in frequent contact with the things of the world should make good use of them without becoming attached to them, for this world and all it contains will pass away." – 1 Corinthians 7:31 NLT.

Questions

1. How can you expand your relationship with God?
2. How can you get God out of the box?
3. How can you not get wrapped up in the worldly things?

Five

A Godly Love Life

I want you to promise, O women [and men] in Jerusalem, not to awaken love, until the time is right. — Song of Solomon 8:4 NLT

Love is patient, love is kind. It does not envy, it does not boast, it is not proud. It is not rude, it is not self-seeking, it is not easily angered, and it keeps no record of wrongs. Love does not delight in evil but rejoices with the truth. It always protects always trusts, always hopes, always preserves. Love never fails... — 1 Corinthians 13:4-8a NIV

...A man will leave his father and mother and be united to his wife, and they will become one flesh. — Genesis 2:24 NIV

Flee from sexual immorality. All other sins a man commits are outside his body, but he who sins sexually sins against his own body. —1 Corinthians 6:18 NIV

God calls us to live pure and Godly lives, so how do we do that? We start by looking at purity. What is purity? The definition of pure is free from anything that damages, weakens, or contaminates. Therefore if we have sin in our life then we are not pure. We need to clean all the sinful nature out of our lives by asking God to come into our hearts and clean them; then once that's done, we must <u>keep</u> our hearts clean. *"For God*

You must commit your purity to God.

Jacob E. Wilcox

did not call us to be impure, but to live a holy life." – 1 Thessalonians 4:7 NIV.

So how do we keep a pure life? It starts with the eyes. The eyes are the doorways to our hearts, so by guarding your eyes you can keep a lot of the impurity out.

Impurity doesn't just come through the eyes, it also comes through the ears. If you're around people that curse a lot and say bad things then your ears will start to soak in the bad language and your brain will start to use that language in your thoughts or speech. So not only guard your eyes but guard your ears too.

So how can we remain pure in our love life? First, I need to say that the "love" that you feel for your boy/girl friend is not actual love, it is infatuation. What's infatuation? It's "to arouse an extravagant or foolish love." You may ask "what's the difference between love and infatuation?" Infatuation is just an emotion while love is a genuine commitment of one's heart mind and soul to another person. Love is not infatuation.

> *"For I resolved to know nothing while I was with you except Jesus Christ and Him crucified."*
> *– 1 Corinthians 2:2 NIV*

Infatuation is weakened by time and separation. Love is strengthened by time and separation. Love involves emotion and the will or the desire and emotional drive to a commitment level.

Marriage

Blessed are the pure in heart, for they shall see God. – Matthew 5:8 KJV.

We need to remember that God wants us to be pure before marriage. He also wants you to pick the spouse that He has chosen for you. (When He chooses a spouse, He chooses correctly.)

He doesn't want you to marry someone with different beliefs as you.

> You must know nothing except His standards for your purity.

The Bible says in 1 Corinthians 6:14: *"Do not be yoked together with unbelievers. For what do righteousness and wickedness have in common? Or what fellowship can light have with darkness."* So don't marry an unbeliever expecting that he or she will change to a Christian afterwards. There's a greater chance that you will turn from your faith that way.

Let God choose your mate; but for Him to show you the one that He wants you to marry you must stay in communication with Him. Just like I said earlier in this book, prayer is essential, so keep praying for the right person to come into your love life.

Something you should really watch for is when you get "caught up in the moment." People can say some very flattering stuff, they can entice you, and they tempt you (sometimes you put yourself in the "moment").

Don't get caught up in the moment; you need to think before you speak and before you do anything. If someone wants you to do something, then think: is what they want me to do going to interfere with God's plan?

It's very easy as young adults to get caught up in the moment that we forget to ask God for guidance. So pay attention to what God's trying to tell you/ He could very much be warning you to stay away from a certain person.

"The time that remains is very short, so husbands should not let marriage be their major concern." – *1 Corinthians 7:29 NLT.*

"God gives some the gift of marriage, and to others He gives the gift of singleness." – *1ˢᵗ Corinthians 7:7 NLT.*

You don't have to marry, or date, for that matter. It's not sinful or shameful to be single; as long as you are doing the Lord's work. *"Happiness or sadness or wealth should not keep anyone from doing God's work."* – *1 Corinthians 7:30 NLT.*

God wants us to do His will, so nothing should hinder or get in the way of that. In <u>certain</u> cases marriage can hinder someone's spiritual walk with Christ.

We are all here for a purpose and God wants us to pursue it

without being hindered by anything. Like I just said, marriage can very much hinder your relationship with Christ if it's not a Christ-centered relationship.

Boundaries

Maybe you are at the age where you don't think about actually marrying someone; maybe you are just attracted to him or her and want to spend more time with this person. That's okay to a certain extent. You should not get physically involved with this person's body. You need to set up limits or boundaries (even if you are single or not). For instance, you need to set a curfew so that you don't stay up late nights with this certain someone. Maybe you should only hang out with this person in a group setting like church, youth group, school, etc.

God calls us to be pure, but you can't be pure when you are spending too much "alone" time with this person. Even if nothing's happening you must not put yourself in the position to sin.

> Abandon your love life to the will of the Father and accept only His best for you. – (Padgett, p. 149)

When you are with this person that you are attracted to, something is bound to happen. It's human nature to want a physical involvement with another human being.

So work on setting or strengthening your boundaries. Don't ever cross your boundaries; and don't ever justify yourself crossing your boundaries. That's only Satan speaking to you. Your boundaries can be the two I mentioned earlier, or they could be others like not kissing or hugging or hand holding. These are just boundaries that God has mentioned to me about. If you don't know what specific boundaries you want in your life, then I would recommend talking to a trusted pastor or adult about boundaries in your life that need re-adjustment.

Values/morals

What are your values? What do you value most in life? It is wise to find someone with the same values and morals as you. If you are a Christian and the person you are attracted to is an atheist, then that won't work out very well. It will either end with one or the other switching sides, or the ending of a relationship with deep scars or secrets. You might have heard the term "secrets don't make friends." Well that's extremely true, especially in relationships. Secrets are never a good thing in a relationship.

Your values are very important, they are the fundamentals of your life, and cannot just be tossed aside. They must be strengthened and encouraged. After all, your values show what kind of life you are living. Do your values show that you are a Christian?

Dating

If you are in your early teens then don't plan on marrying your boy/girl friend; people change over a period of time. The person you really like now could be such a different person later on in life. The reason I am saying this is that most individuals think they are going to marry their boy/girl friend and live happily ever after with rainbows and butterflies. But when the relationship starts to crumble, the individual tries to keep it going even though it isn't working out.

This individual thinks that they have to do something extraordinary to spark the fire again. So they "reset" their standards or boundaries. And maybe that works, but only for a little while.

You need to learn to let it go. Don't get emotionally or physically involved with this person. Stay clear of the "moments."

There are a deal of youth that I have come across who gave too much of their heart away in hope to start the fire again in their

> Remain aware that you may be handling someone else's future spouse. – (Padgett, p. 150)

relationship. But when it failed and they separated, the part of their heart that they had given to that person went with the other person. When that happens we lose our worth; we think we are not good enough and get depressed. Then we repeat the process with the next relationship.

So how can you know you are with the right person? Think: 1. Is this person pushing you across your "pure" boundaries? 2. Does this person believe the same as you?

The best thing possible to do is talk with God about this person that you are attracted to. Maybe you can even talk to your significant other about the problem; maybe they just don't understand there's a problem so mention it to them.

If you are already in a relationship that has already or is going too far physically and emotionally, then you must end it. It will be hard, but God has a plan, and that person will just be a stumbling block for your faith.

Put God first in every area of your life.

Questions

1. What is purity?
2. What is infatuation?
3. How can we guard our eyes?
4. What are ways you can avoid getting "caught up" in the moment?
5. Is God trying to tell you something?

Six

What's Your Mission?

For I know the plans I have for you, declares the Lord,
plans to prosper you and not to harm you,
plansto give you hope and a future.
— Jeremiah 29:11 NIV

"Happiness or sadness or wealth should not keep anyone
from doing God's Work." — 1 Corinthians 7:30 NLT

"Any time you have an opportunity to make a difference in this
world and you don't, then you are wasting your time on earth."
— Roberto Clemente, 1934-1972

What's your mission? What's your calling? Have you ever thought about what you are going to do when you get older; what you want to accomplish?

Believe it or not, but God has a specific job/mission for you; whether it's being a doctor or cleaning toilets at a school. Whatever it is or may be, God has put you there or will put you there on purpose.

> "In achieving success, backbone is more important than wishbone."
> – Frank Tyger

If you have a job or are about to get one you need to work at that job with diligence. Don't get lazy! Work hard at that job, even if you're cleaning toilets, work hard at it. Even if you have nothing to do then go and find something to do, like sweep the floor or move boxes but do something.

Use the time you have at work to talk to others about Jesus. God has given you the opportunity to talk about Jesus with your co-workers, so don't waste it.

If you're not working anytime soon, then find your God-given talent. God has gifted you with something; whether that's cooking, singing, dancing, sports, etc. Use your talents for Jesus while you are still young and have energy.

If you are good at public speaking then use it in your church or somewhere else. People will listen to a young person "preach" because it's unique; any adult can preach or teach. A teen doing it will make people more interested. Why? Because like I just said, it's unique. We don't see very many teens stepping into leading positions (at least I haven't). When you step into a leading position you inspire other teens. You could be the spark that sets off a chain reaction!

> God found Gideon in a hole. He found Joseph in a prison. He found Daniel in a lion's den. Next time you feel unqualified to be used by God remember this. He tends to recruit from the pit not the pedestal.
> – Jon Acuff.

We think sometimes that church is where adults go to hear other adults talk or preach, but that's not it. Christianity is for everyone, from the littlest of children to the oldest of men. So use your talents in and out of the church.

So what is your mission? Here are three questions I want you to ask yourself to determine if you are fulfilling your mission: 1. What kind of impact are you having on others? You could very well be blowing out that spark in someone else's life. 2. Are you moving forward

> We pray about what we want God to do for us. What If we prayed more about what we could do for God? – Craig Groeschel

with your relationship with God? Like I said earlier keeping a strong connection with God is essential. 3. Are you fulfilling your mission? We all have a purpose; we are all called to a mission. You just need to find it and start chasing after it. Make it a priority in your life. *"Whether you eat, drink, or whatsoever you do, do all to the glory of God." – 1 Corinthians 10:31 NIV.*

"Make it your ambition to lead a quiet life, to mind your own business and to work with your hands, just as we told you, so that your daily life may win the respect of outsiders and so that you will not be dependent on anybody." – 1 Thessalonians 4:11-12 NIV. Wow! I think everyone needs to read that verse, don't you think? The last part of the verse is so simple. The only person we are to be dependent on is God, not the government, the schools, the grocery store or anything else.

Part Two

LIFE'S UNEXPECTED PROBLEMS

Seven

The Power of Temptation

No temptation has seized you except what is common to man. And God is faithful; he will not let you be tempted beyond what you can bear. But when you are tempted, he will also provide a way out so that you can stand under it. – 1 Corinthians 10:13 NIV

For our struggle is not against flesh and blood, but against the rulers, against the authorities, against the powers of this dark world and against the spiritual forces of evil in the heavenly realms. – Ephesians 6:12 NIV

Don't be fooled, bad company corrupts good character. – 1 Corinthians 15:33 NIV

Now I'm pretty sure everyone has been tempted before; whether it was being tempted to do something wrong or say something bad (or even thinking something that is displeasing to God).

We must not let these temptations rule our life. Christians must deal with these temptations now. How? Well, you start by assessing the situation. You can use the: who, what, when, why, and how method. Who is the person that's tempting you? What is the temptation?

> Satan tempted man to live out of his own resources. Yielding to this temptation became humanity's downfall.

31

When do you get tempted or when are you most vulnerable? Why does the temptation start and how can you keep from it? Those are the questions you need to ask yourself.

As I was researching this chapter I came across this really good quote that pretty much sums it up: "Keep as far as you can from those temptations that feed and strengthen the sins which you would overcome. Lay siege to your sins, and starve them out, by keeping away the food and fuel which is their maintenance and life." – Author Unknown.

You need to stay away from those temptations. If the temptation is a bad TV show or movie, then stay away from the TV at that certain place and time. If the temptation is a person, place or thing, then stay away from that certain person, place or thing.

It will be hard at first and possibly throughout, and you might even lose friends, but it is worth it in the long run. "For whosoever shall be ashamed of Me and of My words, of him shall the Son of man be ashamed, when he shall come in his own glory, and in his fathers, and of the holy angels." – Luke 9:26 KJV.

> Despite our failure our faith is not in Jeopardy. Trust God and allow Him to fight your battles for you.

You cannot be ashamed of Him. You must stand up for what you believe and resist temptation. I know it won't always work – we are all human we stumble and fall, but don't let failure bring you down. You need to just get right back up and fight even harder. You must have faith in God that He will help you up and fight with you. Watch and pray so that you will not fall into temptation. The spirit is willing, but the body is weak. –Matthew 26:41 NIV.

> God has provided all the resources needed to stand against the craftiness of the devil. – Steve Queen. 2016

Fighting temptation

If we confess our sins, He is faithful and just and will forgive us our sins and purify us from all unrighteousness. – 1 John 1:9 NIV

When tempted, no one should say, "God is tempting me." For God cannot be tempted by evil, nor does He tempt anyone; but each one is tempted when, by his own evil desire, he is dragged away and enticed. Then, after desire has conceived, it gives birth to sin; and sin, when it is full-grown, gives birth to death. – James 1:13-14 NIV

Consider it pure joy, my brothers, whenever you face trials of many kinds, because you know that the testing of your faith develops perseverance. Perseverance must finish its work so that you may be mature and complete, not lacking anything. If any of you lacks wisdom, he should ask God, who gives generously to all without finding fault, and it will be given to him. But when he asks, he must believe and not doubt, because he who doubts is like a wave of the sea, blown and tossed by the wind. – James 1:2-6 NIV

Next time, when you're in the midst of a battle, think things that are true, honest, just, pure, lovely, and of good report, things that are righteous and praiseworthy, think "is this something that I can bring into the presence of God?" If not, then get rid of it.

Like I said earlier, you must guard your eyes. Your eyes are the doorways to your heart. Therefore whatever you see will go straight to your heart, and if you allow enough mess in your heart it will start to kill you inside.

"Be strong in the Lord and His mighty power. Put on the full armor of God so that you can take your stand against the devil's schemes." – Ephesians 6:10-11 NIV.

So above all guard your eyes; turn your gaze away from temptation. If you are being tempted just say a little prayer

> Temptation is not a sin. – Steve Queen, 2016

to God, and ask Him to help you fight the temptation and He will give you strength and/or a way out.

You just have to make the choice if you want to take His path or not. Like I said earlier you will stumble and fall sometimes, but you cannot give up! Just remember that God forgives the humble in heart.

Questions

1. How can you fight temptations on a daily basis?
2. Who is the person tempting you?
3. What is the temptation?
4. When do you get tempted?
5. When are you most vulnerable?
6. Why does the temptation start?

Eight

Peer Pressure

Flee the evil desires of youth, and pursue righteousness, faith, love and peace, along with those who call on the Lord out of a pure heart. Don't have anything to do with foolish and stupid arguments, because you know they produce quarrels. And the Lord's servant must not quarrel; instead, he must be kind to everyone, able to teach, not resentful... They [us] will come to their senses and escape from the trap of the devil, who has taken them captive to do his will. — 2 Timothy 2:22-24, 26 NIV

Now then, my sons listen to me; blessed are those who keep my ways. Listen to my instruction and be wise; do not ignore it.
— Proverbs 8:32-33 NIV

He gives strength to the weary and increases the power of the weak. Even youths grow tired and weary, and young men stumble and fall; but those who hope in the Lord will renew their strength. They will soar on wings like eagles; they will run and not grow weary, they will walk and not be faint. — Isaiah 40:29-31 NIV

The Lord is good, a refuge in times of trouble. He cares for those who trust in Him. — Nahum 1:7 NIV

My sons, if sinners entice you, do not give in to them.
— Proverbs 1:10 NIV

Let us behave properly as in the day, not in carousing and drunkenness, not in sexual promiscuity and sensuality, not in strife and jealousy. But put on the Lord Jesus Christ and make no provision for the flesh in regard to its lusts. – Roman 13:13-14 NASB

Negative peer pressure is another form of temptation. Peer pressure is actually easier for Christians to resist than it is for non-Christians. It may not seem so at first glance because Christians have a higher moral standard than non-Christians; which should put more pressure on us. But Christians also have a greater sense of right and wrong; so their values sometimes allow them to say no quickly to anything that is wrong.

As Christians we have the strongest person on our side: God! When you take a stand for what's right, you are taking a stand for God; and God's side is always the winning side. Christians do have it easier, because God promises never to abandon us.

It might not look like it's easier because Satan doesn't pressure unsaved people like he does Christians. Why? Unsaved people pose no threat to him. Satan will try to get a Christian to turn to alcohol, pornography, drugs, etc.

The Bible says in James 4:7 *"Obey God, Resist the devil and he will flee from you."* Therefore Christians can resist peer pressure, only if we try. But sometimes we don't want to try; sometimes we like the wrong that we do.

It's pleasurable.

It's fun.

It seems "normal."

We live in a fallen world where sin is praised or justified, and the right is persecuted or isolated. The whole system of right and wrong has been dramatically switched up. *"For am I now seeking the favor of men, or of God? Or am I striving to please men? If I were still trying to please men, I would not be a bond-servant of Christ." Galatians 1:10,*

NASB. Paul is speaking the truth in this verse. We are not here to please men, we are here to please God.

"For what will it profit a man if he gains the whole world and forfeits his soul? Or what will a man give in exchange for his soul?" – *Matthew 16:26 NASB*.

There are so many people pressuring us to act like this, to dress like that, to talk a certain way, to be politically correct. Therefore we must exercise our body to stand under all this peer pressure that's on top of us. It will not be easy but once you get a spiritual "beachhead" in your life you can make it through it.

On June 6, 1944, the Allies landed on the beaches of Normandy in France. Soldiers from every walk of life, Canadian, American, British, African etc., fought what seemed like a never ending war.

Death was everywhere.

They fought for every square inch on the beaches; many died. But you know what? Those soldiers held on to every inch of sand and finally got a firm beachhead established. They had a strong beachhead which repelled any counterattacks. Once the Allies got their "foot" in the "door" they went on to conquer Hitler and his Nazi regime.

You need to take some advice from the invasion of France. You need to land your spiritual warriors on the beaches of temptation, depression, self-harm, pornography, or any other situation you might have. This tactic is not just for peer pressure; it's for everything.

Fight for every inch. How? Memorizing scripture is a start; also finding positive influences; which I'll talk about later.

You might be thinking: all this stuff about "beachheads" and spiritual warriors sound crazy, but just think about it spiritually. It works; I've done it before. You just got to give it a chance. But you can't invade half-heartedly, you need to be all-in spiritually and physically.

You know even Jesus was tempted, but not successfully. He was tempted by Satan: *"Then Jesus was led up by the spirit into the desert to be tempted by the devil."* – *Matthew 4:1 NIV*; by the Pharisees *"The Pharisees also with the Sadducees came, and tempting desired Him that*

He would shew them a sign from heaven." – Matthew 16:1 KJV; and even Peter put pressure on Him (Matthew 16:22). But He never gave into the peer pressure.

The prophet Daniel and his three friends is another good example of dealing with peer pressure. Daniel and his three friends were taken captive by the king of Babylon, but always resisted their captor's pressure to worship idols and false God's. On one occasion, the king threatened to throw them in a fiery furnace if they didn't worship the golden image. They resisted and God protected them while they were in the furnace. *"…The Lord knoweth how to deliver the godly out of temptations…" – 2 Peter 2:9 KJV.*

So I've talked about some famous people who resisted peer pressure. So what are ways you can deal with peer pressure? Here are some things you can do when peer pressure comes your way:

1. Pray and ask God for wisdom and guidance.
2. If someone wants you to do something say: "I'm sorry, that's against my religion."
3. Find someone with the same values and beliefs as you; it's better to have a partner with you to help.
4. Ask someone older and wiser on how to deal with a specific peer pressure.

Those are just a few ways we can deal with peer pressure. Above all trust that God will get you out of the situation if you just ask Him.

In 2 Peter 2:9 we read that the Lord knows how to rescue the godly from temptation and in 1 Corinthians 10:13 tells us that God won't allow temptation beyond what we can resist.

God can deliver us from temptation and negative peer pressure if we pray for it. But we should also pray that peer pressure does not arise. If it does, say no quickly. Even if the results from doing right don't seem promising; they will turn out for the best in the end. Don't conform to the world; transform to the will of God.

Youth are also very much pressured by society. Society tells us to wear a certain style of clothing or talk a certain way and if you don't you won't fit in and when you don't fit in you get picked on and bullied. *"Do not be conformed to this world, but be transformed by the renewing of your mind, so that you may prove what the will of God is, that which is good and acceptable and perfect."* – Romans 12:2 NLT.

This is a major problem with young adults. Society is pressuring us to go to school, get good grades, get a job, and act a certain way. Society is pressuring us every single day.

Like I addressed earlier, we need to remember that Christians don't blend in with the world – we stand out physically and mentally.

Even sometimes the church puts pressure on us to be a godly person or to excel in the Bible studies.

So in conclusion, don't let society govern your life, be free and trust God! Live a free Godly life.

Questions

1. How can we stay clear of peer pressure?
2. How can we not put pressure on others?

Nine

Depression

The righteous cry out and the Lord hears them; He delivers them from all their troubles. The Lord is close to the brokenhearted and saves those who are crushed in spirit. — Psalms 34:17-18 NIV

Come to me, all who are weary and heavy laden, and I will give you rest. — Matthew 11:28 NASB

Cast all your anxiety on Him, because he cares for you. — 1st Peter 5:7 NIV

Fear thou not; for I am with thee; be not dismayed; for I am thy God; I will strengthen thee; yea I will help thee; yea, I will uphold thee with the right hand of my righteousness. — Isaiah 41:10 KJV

Before I start talking about ways you can get rid of depression, I want to define depressed. The American Heritage Dictionary defines depressed in two definitions. 1. Low in spirits, dejected. 2. Suffering from psychological depression.

Everyone experiences the first one at some time in their life. We all get sad, whether you're sad about failing a test or an ended relationship. Whatever it may be you can take comfort in knowing that it will likely pass in a short time.

In the meantime, keep attending church, keep in contact with

Christ, and keep reading the scripture. (Psalms is good for when you're down.) Don't spend too much time thinking about the things that brings sadness, or it will take you captive and continually make you depressed.

So what about "psychological" depression? Certainly you need to be doing the things in the first one. But if you have it you should see a professional, because this type of depression is very real illness, just as real as cancer or the flu.

Clinical depression is often caused by a chemical imbalance in the brain. It's not "just in your mind." Depression is usually treatable with a combination of medicine and counseling. Unfortunately, less than half of depressed people seek treatment. People resist treatment because they believe depression isn't serious, that they can treat it themselves, or that it is a personal weakness rather than a serious medical illness.

Being depressed is simply being in a low point or low state physically or emotionally. As young adults as we go through the physical and emotional changes in our lives, we can often feel down. Sometimes combinations of physical and social difficulties or changes cause some of us to draw into ourselves. Other times we only see the negative things that surround us and this can makes us depressed. Like I said earlier, these physical, emotional and social circumstances are very real, there's no question about the reality of these issues in our lives.

> *"His own iniquities will capture the wicked, and he will be held with the cords of his sin. — Proverbs 5:22 NASB*

So how should we handle all these physical, emotional and social circumstances? Let us first deal with the physical lows that people, especially young adults, can go through.

So you find yourself trapped in a body that seems to be changing at lightning speed. Many new things are happening, new appearances, new feelings, and new problems like acne for some (I know by experience how acne can affect the life of a teen). This is

Jacob E. Wilcox

a very unpleasant change that seems to rule the life of us teenagers, but even this will pass.

Just don't get down about this stuff. So often when we start to change we begin focusing on ourselves. All we can see is our own problems, our own changes, and our very real issues. But if we don't change our perspective on the issues, it can lead us to only focus on all the negative things instead of the positive things.

We get depressed because we put our focus on the negative stuff that happens in our life. When you focus on the bad you won't see the good that God is trying to show you. You'll miss out on the wonderful blessings that He gives you; so don't focus on the bad stuff. I've trained myself to focus on only the good things, and it gives me joy.

I was once asked why I smiled so much. I simply told them that it's because I see all the many blessings that God has given me because I look. It doesn't have to be some big miracle, just the small things like warm clothes, a roof over your head, food to eat, friends etc. Whatever it may be, when you start giving thanks, you'll stop being depressed. Make it a habit to view your cup as half full, not half empty! So much of our happiness depends on our perspective. Let it be a Godly perspective. Think about Paul and Silas, they were in a cold, dark, smelly prison with their hands and feet in uncomfortable shackles. What did they do? They sang songs, prayed, and soon they had an opportunity to lead a whole family to Christ. They certainly had every reason to complain. Yet, at the same time they had more reasons to rejoice.

> "Do you not know that your body is a temple of the Holy Spirit who is in you, whom you have received from God? You are not your own, you were bought at a price. Therefore honor God with your body." – 1 Corinthians 6:19-20 NIV

Think about it. Don't you have more reasons to rejoice as a young Christian than you have reasons to complain? Besides, to complain is to complain against God for the conditions He's allowed you to be in for the moment. To complain is to be unthankful to God! If you're a Christian teen you have a lot to be thankful for and your life and attitude needs to show it. If you are a child of God, as mad and depressed as you

> Depression is really the mishandling of life's problems.

get, you cannot remove the guilt that the Holy Spirit brings down on you. The only way to be happy when you're a Christian is to do right. I believe the most miserable and depressed people on Earth are Christians living in disobedience, because unlike an unbeliever that is insensitive to God, the true Christian has a sensitive heart towards God and they feel the guilt and lack of close fellowship with God.

Depression is really the mishandling of life's problems and situations, some of which, people bring on themselves. We're all going to have difficulties and problems come our way.

How do we respond to these problems and difficulties? Depression, because of spiritual problems, is like being caught in the "spider's web of your own sin." The only way out is to deal with the sin that entraps you! Let's look at some examples that a typical teen may encounter.

1: You're depressed because of your parents' rules or standards.

You've responded unbiblically to God and your parents. Ephesians 6:1 says: *"Children, obey your parents in the Lord, for this is right."* There's no wiggle room when it comes to obedience to your parents. There's no in-between, it's either obedience or disobedience on your part. Your depression, that you're blaming on your parents' rules, really has little to do with your parents' standards, but has everything to do with your wrong response towards your parents, which is a sinful response. In this case, you've

> May we never let the things we can't have, or don't have, spoil our enjoyment of the things we do have and can have. – Richard L. Evans.

disobeyed God first, for He gave the command for children to obey their parents. Parents don't make rules because they hate you; as a matter of fact it's the complete opposite. Parents draw lines and dictate rules because they love you and they don't want you doing things you might regret in the future. They discipline us because they want us to grow in maturity. If a parent doesn't discipline and teach their child then that child will grow up knowing no boundaries and having no respect for people in authority; therefore they become violent to society.

I am blessed to have parents who raised me with rules and boundaries. It's only because of their strict rules, that I am the way I am. Without my parents' Godly discipline and authority I would've never experienced God the way I do. I would've never gone to church. I would've written this book. I would be submersed in sin and disobedience.

If you've been complaining about Dad and Mom's rules, confess it, then apologize to your parents and see what happens when your relationship with God and your parents is right. You begin to be a much happier teen! However, if you continue to do wrong, plan on being depressed more and more, because you're choosing to respond unbiblically towards your problems and circumstances.

2: You're upset because your boyfriend or girlfriend broke up with you or things are not going well with the relationship.

You're not content in being single and pure until you're ready for a marriage commitment for life. You want the world's way of dating rather than God's principles and commands of finding a spouse and remaining pure while you're looking.

First, is the relationship biblical to begin with? Does God want you to have the type of relationship you're having with this guy or girl? Are you getting more involved emotionally or physically than you should be? Have you sinned in the process of having this relationship? Depression over boyfriend/girlfriend struggles is common, but does God want Christians following the world's way in this area? Biblically, teens should not be doing anything that is only intended for married couples to be involved in, including developing emotional attachments or physical attachments which you will learn later in this book. Often Christians will directly or indirectly make a promise of commitment to another, and then later break off the commitment. Making promises or vows is a serious issue in God's perspective – and it should be with teens also. I believe that God is angered at the turmoil teens put themselves in when following the world's way of dating, which involves so many break ups and breaking of vows. The solution to dating depression is to obey God's Word and to remain pure in every area of life. Any other approach will set you up to sin and for future depression and perhaps marriage problems when you do finally get married. If you are still uncertain about this, then I would suggest going back to "A Godly Love Life" or "premarital sex" chapter and read it.

3: You don't like your life, the way you look, where you live, the parents God gave you, the church you're in etc.

You've responded unbiblically to God's provision. Learning to be content and happy with what you have is the proper response. God always knows what you have, whether it's your money, your home, your parents, or your church. God is never surprised at these things, because He's provided them. If you're mad at what you have, then you're really angry at God and you're not content with what He's

> Everyone wants happiness. No one wants pain. But you can't have a rainbow without a little rain. – Author unknown

given you. *"...for I have learned to be content in whatever circumstances I am."* – Philippians 4:11 NASB. *"If we have food and covering, with these we shall be content."* – 1 Timothy 6:8 NASB.

There are people that are so disfigured from birth defects or accidents, yet they're happy to be alive. People like this are not focusing on "what they don't have," but on what they do have. Like

I said earlier, if you're depressed about what you don't have, start being thankful for what you do have; when you start giving thanks for what you have in life, then you should stop being depressed! So much of our happiness depends on our perspective. Let it be a godly perspective! *"Giving thanks always for all things unto God and the Father in the name of our Lord Jesus Christ."* – Ephesians 5:20 KJV.

Other than genuine physical issues that can cause depression, you hold the key to being happy! You can choose to respond positively and properly to life's problems and circumstances. God sees your every move and thought. Seek to please Him with every response and happiness and joy will surround you. In fact, if you live a life that pleases God, many will come to see your happiness and ask how they can get it for themselves. However, the opposite is true if you continue as a Christian to respond improperly and ignore your sinful responses. Your depression will drive others away. Happiness and joy attract, so do right and be happy!

Questions

1. How can we stay positive during life's tough situations?
2. What can we do to combat depression?
3. Out of every bad situation find at least one good thing?

Ten

Self-harm

Do you not know that you are a temple of God and that the spirit of God dwells in you? If any man destroys the temple of God, God will destroy him. For the temple of God is holy, and that is what you are.
— 1 Corinthians 3:16-17 NASB

You are the sons [daughters] of the Lord your God; you shall not cut yourselves nor shave your foreheads for the sake of the dead. — Deuteronomy 14:1 NASB

Self-harm sometimes seems like it's the only way out; that physical pain is so much easier to deal with than emotional for physical pain heals, whereas emotional pain leaves scars that can't be treated, scars that never fade. Then again some people self-harm for attention. They believe that it's "cool" to be so depressed, that the world might recognize them and give them attention.

Self-harm, self-mutilation, or self-abuse, is defined as the deliberate, repetitive, impulsive harming of one's self. Believe it or not but cutting is pretty common; those who struggle are not alone in this. Many teens and even adults hurt themselves physically as a way to try and relieve the emotional pain that is taking over their lives. Cutting is a behavior that stems from depression, which is a much deeper problem than the marks in your skin.

Self-injury is considered to be an addiction, and it's not easy to just stop. Behaviors include but aren't limited to: cutting, burning, picking or interfering with a wound healing, infecting one's self, punching/hitting, inserting objects into skin, bruising or breaking bones, and forms of hair pulling.

Self*harm isn't pleasing to God because the attitude behind it does not glorify Him. All people are created in the image of God. *"So God created man in His own image; in the image of God He created them." Genesis 1:27 NKJV.*

All people are valuable to God because they are meant to reflect God's image. Self-harm devalues that image. It ultimately says through our attitude that God is of little value to us or that we are of little value to God. This couldn't be any further from the truth! But yes, I know school is very stressful. Work can be stressful, friendships can be stressful. We have a lot going on in life. Sometimes, the emotional pain is unbearable. Relief would be fantastic at some points. But that doesn't mean every outlet for relief is right or healthy. If you cut to relieve depression, you're opening not only your flesh, but the possibility to be hurt inside even more!

Here's what the Bible says about self-harm. In the Old Testament cutting of skin was used mainly in practice of false religions. 1 Kings 18: 24-29 talks about the worship of Baal. Elijah invited worshippers to test their false god, but when Baal did not prove any power, *"they cried aloud and cut themselves after their custom with swords and lances, until blood gushed out."* Even though it was "normal" in the Old Testament, God established a rule against the practice. Leviticus 19:28 NKJV says, *"you shall not make any cutting in your flesh for the dead, nor tattoo any marks on you; I am the Lord."*

It's not only a stress relief but also a cry for someone to notice that something is wrong in their lives. A guy or girl who hurts themselves may feel empty, lonely, fearful, or is unable to express his or her feelings. The act may have been brought out because of past abuse or depression. Cutting is a result of deeper issue within the heart, and if you know someone who cuts then have compassion on them. They are struggling and don't know how else to deal with their pain. God wants to heal them, and you can help. Galatians 6:2 says *"bear one another's burdens."* Love your friend and show them that they matter to you and to God.

If you are struggling with self-harm yourself, please find help in a trusted teen or adult. Even though these actions may seem like they help, they could eventually develop into even greater struggles like addictions to drugs, or even eating disorders. In fact, you may be dealing with some of that right now; but you don't have to suffer alone. You have the power to make the choice to seek help and recover. *"The righteous cry, and the Lord hears and delivers them out of all their troubles. The Lord is near to the brokenhearted and saves those who are crushed in spirit."* – Psalms 34:17-18 NASB.

Cutting very often stems from a very low view of self, seeing yourself as worthless or invisible, which is totally countered and met by the reality of God's love. Listen to the words of Jesus in Matthew 11:28-30 NKJV: *"Come to me, all you who labor and are heavy laden, and I will give you rest. Take My yoke upon you and learn from Me, for I am gentle and lowly in heart, and you will find rest for your souls, for My yoke is easy and My burden is light."* People are valuable because Jesus died in their place. Self-harm is always wrong as it denies the value of God places on us.

If you have a friend who is struggling with self-harm because of depression or something else just be there for them, stick with them encourage them to stop, make them laugh, don't leave them. *"And be kind to one another, tenderhearted, forgiving one another, even as God in Christ forgave you."* – Ephesians 4:32 NKJV.

If you are dealing with it, then focus on those to whom you mean the world; those people do exist. They're always going to be someone who needs you in their life, who adores you. Focus on them, not those to whom you mean nothing for those people are irrelevant. While all addictions are hard to overcome, help and treatment are out there and available. Recovery and freedom are possible. No matter what you're wrestling with: self-harm, depression, drugs, body image issues, sexual addictions, or other areas of brokenness, God can heal all things if you just ask Him.

> *"Confess your sins to each other and pray for each other so that you may be healed. The earnest prayer of a righteous person has great power and wonderful results." – James 5:16 NLT*

> *"Therefore we do not lose heart. Even though our outward man is perishing, yet the inward man is being renewed day by day."*
> *– 2 Corinthians 4:16 NKJV*

Question

1. How can you help a friend who self-harms?

Eleven

Suicide

"Today I have given you the choice between life and death, between blessings and curses. Now I call on heaven and earth to witness the choice you make. Oh, that you would choose life, so that you and your descendants might live! You can make this choice by loving the Lord your God, obeying Him, and committing yourself firmly to Him. This is the key to your life..."
– Deuteronomy 30:9-20 NIV

Suicide is the act of intentionally taking one's own life, or as some have called it, "self murder." The Bible views suicide as equal to murder, which is what it is – self murder. God is the only one who is to decide when, where, and how a person should die. *"My whole life is in your hands. Save me from my enemies. Save me from those who are chasing me." – Psalms 31:15 NIV.*

The Bible mentions six specific people who committed suicide: Abimelech: *"He said to his young armor bearer, 'draw your sword and kill me! Don't let it be said that a woman killed Abimelech!' So the young man stabbed him with his sword, and he died." – Judges 9:54 NLT.* Saul and his armor bearer: *"Saul groaned to his armor bearer, 'take your sword and kill me before these pagan philistines run me through and humiliate me.' But his armor bearer was afraid and would not do it. So Saul took his own sword and fell on it. When his armor bearer realized that Saul was dead, he fell on his own sword and died* beside the king." *1 Samuel 31:4-5 NLT.* Ahithophel: *"...Ahithophel was publicly disgraced when Absalom refused his advice. So he saddled his donkey, went to his hometown, set his affairs in order, and hanged himself..." – 2 Samuel 17:23 NLT.* Zimri: *"When Zimri saw that the city had been taken, he went into the citadel of the king's house and burned it down over himself and died in the flames." – 1 Kings 16:18 NLT.* And Judas: *"So Judas threw the money into the temple and left. Then he went away and hanged himself." – Matthew 27:5 NIV.*

Some people consider Samson's death an instance of suicide, because he knew his actions would lead to death, but Samson's goal was to kill Philistines, not himself.

In other cases some people in scripture felt deep despair in life. Solomon, in his pursuit of pleasure, reached the point where he "hated life." *"So I hated life. That's because the works that is done on this earth made me sad. None of it has any meaning. It's like chasing the wind." – Ecclesiastes 2:17 NIV.* Jonah was so angry with God that he wanted to die. *"When the sun arose, God sent a burning east wind. The sun beat down on Jonah's head. It made him weak. He wanted to die. So he said, 'I'd rather die than live'." – Jonah 4:8 NIV.* Elijah was fearful and depressed and longed for death. *"Then he traveled for one day into the desert. He came to a small tree. He sat down under it. He prayed that he would die. 'Lord, I've had enough,' he said. 'Take my life. I'm no better than my people of long ago'." – 1 Kings 19:4 NIV.*

> Even though we experience loss in our life, our hope is not gone.

However, none of these men committed suicide. Solomon learned to *"fear God and keep his commandments, for this is the duty of all mankind." – Ecclesiastes 12:3 NIV.* Jonah received rebuke from God. Elijah was confronted by an angel, and was allowed to rest, and

> There's no doubt that suicide is a terrible tragedy. For a Christian it's an even greater tragedy because it is a waste of a life that God intended to use in a glorious way.

was given a new commission. They all learned that, although the pressure they faced was beyond their ability to endure, the Lord can bear all things. *"This happened that we might not rely on ourselves but on God, who raises the dead." – 2 Corinthians 1:9 NIV.*

God is the giver of life. He gives and He takes away. Suicide is ungodly because it rejects God's gift of life. No person should presume to take God's authority upon themselves to end his or her own life. Suicide also has a deep and lasting impact on those left behind; the painful scars left by suicide don't heal easily.

According to the Bible, suicide is a sin. So if it's a sin then does God forgive suicide? Do Christians who commit suicide go to Hell? Sadly, yes. If you commit suicide you are murdering yourself and murder is a sin. So you will spend eternity in Hell for it. It's sad that so many people are committing suicide, thinking that it's better than being here. But it's not better on the other side; it's far worse. So if you know someone who is thinking suicidal thoughts or battling depression, pray for them and spend time with them. Show them how much you really care.

Life will get better either here on Earth or if you're a Christian, in Heaven. Suicide won't get you to Heaven, if that were the case I would have already taken my life.

If you are battling this then pray to God, ask him for strength, then start focusing on the people who love you, they will be broken if you were to commit suicide. Don't wait. Do it now. Break free from the suicidal thoughts and attitudes. Let God fill you up, let Him work in your life. He has a plan for you. He put everyone on this planet for a reason, so therefore you are not a mistake!

Questions

1. How can we stop people from this dangerous thinking and attitudes?
2. What can you do to "restart" your mind to think good thoughts?
3. Is suicide really the answer?

Twelve

Bullying

So do not be afraid. I am with you. Do not be terrified. I am your God. I will make you strong and help you. My powerful right hand will take care of you. I always do what is right. – Isaiah 41:10 NIV

Bullies have often had the stereotype of being a kid larger than the rest of the kids. They also have had the stereotypical bully duties of "stealing lunch money, and sometimes stuffing kids in lockers." But things have changed due to our modern day society. So let's look at our modern day bully. They come in many shapes and sizes and now due to social media they are much more involved in everyday life, and at times nearly impossible to get away from.

Cyber bullying is constantly changing and growing. The majority of students have Facebook, Instagram, text messaging, etc. Bullies these days will often make threats, blackmail and try to intimidate people online.

There is a biblical response to bullying that's practical, and spiritual. However, it's not for the fainthearted or double-minded person to engage. There must be a firm confidence of faith in God to empower you with wisdom in dealing with difficult people.

Many people think that bullying is a bothersome but relatively harmless rite of passage into adulthood. They often paraphrase Friedrich Nietzsche who said "that which does not kill us makes us stronger." The Bible says otherwise. Just talk to a friend who's being bullied, and you'll discover soon enough that they do not feel stronger. If you can get them to talk you'll discover that they feel hopeless, one of the most dangerous states of mind for any person. They hate themselves. During the rare moments when they do talk honestly, what comes out of them is the heavy language of despair, misery, and exasperation. *"Hope deferred makes the heart sick. But a longing fulfilled is the tree of life." – Proverbs 13:12 NIV.*

If you are being bullied online or in person, then here are a few things you can put into action.

1. **Evaluate your relationship with the bully**: Is this a genuine bully, or a friend having a bad day? Have you done something to upset this person? Do you owe this person an apology?

2. **Evaluate the severity of the threats:** Do you feel worried that the person will harm you physically? If you do, you must report it to an older "trustworthy" adult, if it was a text save it, print them out and take them to your parents, or teacher you trust.

3. **Seek wisdom from God on how to deal with the bully.** *"The Lord gives wisdom, and from his mouth come Knowledge and understanding." – Proverbs 2:6 NIV.* Responding in your flesh or carnal nature will be the easiest, yet most unspiritual way of dealing with a bully. Sometimes your past interactions with bullies will make you more defensive and reactive instead of you being thoughtfully proactive in the Spirit. Seeking wisdom from God leaves no lingering regret and plenty of room for grace. Wisdom nurtures a willing heart and an open mind to draw a bully towards a spirit of repentance.

> Your value does not decrease based on someone's inability to see your worth. – Author unknown

4. **Don't get revenge:** *"Do not repay anyone evil for evil. Be careful to do what is right in the eyes of everybody. – Romans 12:17 NIV. "Do not take revenge, my friends, but leave room*

for God's wrath, for it is written: 'It is mine to avenge; I will repay,' says the Lord." – Romans 12:29 NIV.

Forgiving a bully isn't excusing their behavior or allowing them to continue in their abusiveness. Rather, it's more about your heart than theirs. Your heart needs to remain free from bitterness, revenge, or the need for retribution, the Lord will take care of all revenge both small and great. God is a God of justice and will repay every indignity on the heads of those who dare to violate his commandment of loving one another.

5. **Learn and grow from a bully:** *"My brethren, count it all joy, when you fall into various trials, knowing that the testing of your faith produces patience. But let patience have its perfect work, that you may be perfect and complete, lacking in nothing." – James 1:2-4 NKJV.* It is hard to consider bullying "all joy" but think of what you can learn from it, like conflict resolutions, value of words, overcoming obstacles, trust in God, etc.

6. **Learn from other people who have been through it:** *"Plans fail for lack of counsel, but with many advisers they succeed." – Proverbs 15:22 NIV.* Everything in life can teach you a lesson; you just have to be willing to listen and learn. "Hindsight is better than foresight" and many of us have learned this lesson the hard way. Therefore it's good to discuss strategy and insight from people who've dealt with bullies in the past. We can learn to not make repeated mistakes. The body of Christ needs to build a fort of protection around a weaker believer so that their faith in God isn't destroyed by the actions of bullies.

7. Take action when prompted by the Holy Spirit: "Each one should test his own actions..."-Galatians 6:4 NIV. There's no one way to deal with a bully. Every situation can be unique because of the bully, the target, and the situation around the events. What's most important is to cultivate closeness

with God the Father in prayer in preparation for the right and timely action. Sometimes the response to a bully may seem harsh or impractical but yet God's power isn't limited. His purpose and plan will stand when we courageously take

> Every battle will play out with the ultimate victory in Christ Jesus, when you walk by faith and not by sight.

action in faith. These last three are the most important:

Pray for the bully: Sometimes it's obvious the bully has some serious issues, and is in need of help; remember hurt people hurt people. Don't you want to help or at least make them leave you alone? The bully isn't your real enemy. Your enemy is Satan and he will use anyone to get your eyes off God so use the bully to increase your time with God. Keeping a prayerful attitude about a particular bully will keep you sensitive of their lost soul. You never know how God may intervene in the lives of the most bitter, hardened, and evil hearts and change them into the likeness of Christ for the building of God's kingdom. Nothing is too hard for God. *"...I tell you: Love your enemies and pray for those who persecute you. ...He causes his sun to rise on the evil and the good, and sends rain on the righteous and the unrighteous. If you love those who love you, what reward will you get? Are not even the tax collectors doing that? And if you greet only your brothers, what are you doing more than others? Do not even pagans do that?"* – Matthew 5:44-47 NIV.

Move on with life: Try not to obsess or focus too much on what bullies say. Try to move on. The more you let the situations hinder your day to day life, the more you empower the bully. The easiest way to move on is to consider the source. Would you take advice from this person? Is this person constantly in trouble? God has a very specific plan for you. So go get help from Him and friends, family, pastor, etc., so you can keep running your race, and get through the trials that are thrown your way.

Jacob E. Wilcox

Remember how God sees you: You were created in God's image! You are exactly the way He wanted you created, and He has a very specific plan for you! Don't let someone who does not know your purpose stop you from living the life God wants! *"For I know the plans I have for you, declares the lord, plans to prosper you and not to harm you, plans to give you hope and a future." – Jeremiah 29:11 NIV.*

[39] "I tell you, do not resist an evil person. If someone strikes you on the right cheek, turn to him the other also..." [41] "If someone forces you to go one mile, go with him two miles." – Matthew 5: 39, 41 NIV.

Questions

1. How can you deal with your bully?
2. How can you pray for your bully?
3. What would Jesus do about a bully?

Thirteen

Negative Influences

"Do not be mislead: Bad company corrupts good character."
– 1 Corinthians 15:33 NIV.

It is virtually impossible to live a life that is unaffected by other people. Their attitudes and opinions blow into our lives like a cold wind blowing into a warm house when the door is opened. They shape our perspectives and influence our decision making.

> Negative influence isn't always obvious.

When one godly person's life sharpens another's it's a good thing. It yields a harvest of good and mature fruit over time. But I can think of several instances in my life when I allowed the negative influence of others to sway my better judgment. Like many things in life, the moments in which we've been swayed by bad influences are often easier to see with hindsight. We are very vulnerable at being influenced toward ungodly attitudes and actions. The process can be so subtle that sometimes we don't even notice it.

"Do not be mislead: bad company corrupts good character." – 1 Corinthians 15:33 NIV. Given this scripture, how do we recognize and respond to the people in our lives who may indeed be "bad company"? The first step is to identify the people who scripture warns us to beware of.

There are a lot of foolish behaviors we should avoid, I will name a few. Gossip and division: *"A twisted person stirs up fights. Anyone who talks about others comes between close friends." – Proverbs 16:28 NIV.* Anger and violence: *"A man who wants to hurt others tries to get them to sin. He leads them down a path that isn't good." – Proverbs 18:29 NIV.* Lying: *"The Lord hates those who don't keep their word, but he delights in those who do." – Proverbs 12:22 NLT.* And lack of compassion: *"Those who do what is right want to treat poor people fairly. But those who do what is wrong don't care about the poor." – Proverbs 29:7 NIV.* Paul says that we must avoid other forms of influence: *"But now I am writing you that you must not associate with anyone who calls himself a brother but is sexually immoral or greedy, an Idolater or a slanderer, a drunkard or a swindler. With such a man do not even eat." – 1 Corinthians 5:11 NIV.* Paul knew that when people who called themselves Christians surrendered to sinful lifestyles thus dulled their ability to discern right and wrong. *"The Spirit clearly says that in later times some will abandon the faith and follow deceiving spirits and things taught by demons. Such teachings come through hypocritical liars, whose consciences have been seared as with a hot iron." – 1 Timothy 4:1-2 NIV.* They in turn, drew others into their folly.

> "Just because someone is your friend and you are afraid to hurt their feelings, doesn't mean that you have to keep them as a large part of your life. Friends shouldn't be affecting you in a negative way. It is okay to walk away from that friendship. It won't be easy but it will be worth it." -Erika Danver. 2016

Some of the biggest potential enemies to spiritual growth were not those outside the church who were engaged in blatant sin, but those inside it. Again and again, we're warned to be on the lookout for wolves in sheep's clothing, outwardly "spiritual" people who lead God's children astray. *"Don't let anyone deceive you in any way, for that day will not come until the rebellion occurs and man of lawlessness is revealed, the man doomed to destruction. – 2 Thessalonians 2:3 NIV.*

In addition to keeping a watchful eye open for the characters described in scripture above, we must understand how the corrupting power of bad company works and why we sometimes give in. *"Therefore, since we are surrounded by such a great cloud of witnesses, let us throw off everything that hinders and the sin that so easily entangles, and let us run with perseverance the race marked out for us." – Hebrews 12:1 NIV.* It is the nature of sin to trip and entangle us. When we are around those whose lives are immersed in sin we are exposed to its entangling influence. One way is through the appeal of rebellion. We don't like people telling us what to do – we don't even like God telling us what to do. Submitting our livelihood to his leadership is hard for us. The sinful nature of our hearts predisposes us all to rebellion.

Like Adam and Eve in the garden, we are so easily enticed to disobey God through the snakelike influence of bad company.

We are all human, and humans desire a worldly approval, we all crave it, we believe it will validate our worthiness as a person. But when our cravings to please people overshadow our reverence for God, we have allowed the world's influence in our lives to exceed His. And the cost is greater than we can ever imagine.

But yes. I know sin is pleasurable, at least in the beginning. Sin promises to satisfy our deepest longings. Take candy for example. If I was to eat as much candy as I wanted, whenever I wanted (which is often) I would be enjoying the sinful pleasure of gluttony. Eating candy isn't a sin in and of itself: it's my overconsumption of it that makes it a sin. And all sins will find you out. Like when I step on a scale.

We must be vigilant and aware of those who would have me believe the pleasures of sin aren't worth worrying about. If I tell a friend that I need to restrain from eating candy, and they respond, "Oh come on, it's not that big a deal," I need to get away from their negative influence upon me. A lot of times negative influence is obvious because it encourages us to indulge a known weakness. At other times, however, corrupting influence is more subtle. It may not lead to blatantly sinful decisions instead; we may have a little more than a troubling sense that something isn't quite right in this relationship.

So here are some ways to spot that you are being influenced negatively: if you are violating areas of conviction, if you feel consistently heavy-hearted, agitated, or depressed after spending time with this person, if you are rationalizing behavior or thought that you previously avoided, if you're more lax regarding areas of weakness, and if you are making questionable decisions that were never options before. Those signs alert us to the possibility that someone's effect on our lives is pulling us the wrong way.

> Just because a Christian won't support something doesn't mean that they hate the people involved in it.

OK. So you found this certain person who's influencing you negatively, what should you do about this person? This person might be your closest friend, or someone you've been with for years. I don't think there's a set formula for discerning where to establish protective boundaries. Just because someone influences you negatively in one area in your life doesn't mean this person can't make a positive contribution in another. Because of that, you should ask God how He wants you to respond. He promises that He'll give you wisdom when you ask for it. *"If any of you lack wisdom, he should ask God, who gives generously to all without finding fault, and it will be given to him." – James 1:5 NIV.*

They're two major things we need to do about this person. One is limiting our time with this person, and the other is whether or not to communicate with this person about our reasons for limiting contact or ending the relationship. Sometimes talking openly with someone about their negative influence can open the door to a deeper relationship. It might also encourage them to take inventory of their own vulnerabilities. However, there are also times when it's best to act without explanation. For example, if we have concerns about a person's trustworthiness, it's probably better to limit our vulnerability.

While you are limiting the negative input, you also need to submit your life to the positive influence that will protect you. Other godly teens can help you overcome bad influences; they will give you strength and encouragement.

Another thing you need to do is listen and focus on God's truth The Word inoculates our mind against the lies and deception of sin. As we encounter scriptures that address our struggles, our response is to submit ourselves to God in prayer. Through prayer, we allow our hearts, minds, and will to be influenced by the power of the Holy Spirit. One important thing that we should not do is become that negative influence. If a friend is trying to get rid of something in their life, then encourage them, and help them be a Christlike person.

Bad company does corrupt good character. But if we remain honest about our own weaknesses, and if we seek out the protective, positive resources God has graciously given us, we don't have to be drawn into the destructive power of sin. By God's grace, we'll grow in the kind of Christlike influence that He wants us to embody in our relationships. Confession is an important first step; it frees us from false guilt and gives us an opportunity to recommit to pursuing a holy life. Confession also paves the way for others to protect us where we're vulnerable through their ongoing encouragement and support.

Question

1. What are ways we can avoid bad company?

Fourteen

Drug Abuse

Be very careful, then, how you live – not as unwise but as wise,
making the most of every opportunity, because the days are evil.
Therefore do not be foolish, but understand what the Lord's will is.
– Ephesians 5:15-17 NIV

Let us behave decently, as in the daytime, not in orgies and
drunkenness, not in sexual immortality and debauchery,
not in dissension and jealousy. Rather, clothe yourselves
with the Lord Jesus Christ, and do not think about
how to gratify the desires of the sinful nature.
– Romans 13:13 NIV

Do you not know that the wicked will not inherit the kingdom of
God? Do not be deceived: neither the sexually immoral nor idolaters
nor adulterers nor male prostitutes nor homosexual offenders nor
thieves nor the greedy nor drunkards nor slanderers nor swindlers
will inherit the kingdom of God. – 1 Corinthians 6:9-10 NIV

Drug abuse has become a major problem in our society. What does the Bible say about these mind transforming drugs? Is drug use OK?

You probably have heard anti-drug messages before. Maybe you've said, "sure, whatever." There are a lot of attitudes about drug use floating around. Some say it's harmless, while others say it's not. But maybe what you're hearing doesn't add up with what you see. You might know someone who uses drugs, and they do well in school or in sports. Maybe you see them only smoke and drink at parties. It's the same in the media, where many celebrities enthusiastically endorse drugs but seem to suffer no ill effects from their habit.

"Be sober, be vigilant; because your advisor the devil, as a roaring lion, walketh about, seeking whom he may devour." – 1 Peter 5:8 KJV.

Self-destructive, self-indulgent behavior like drug abuse is a sin, there's no "sugar coating" it. It is a perversion of God's plan, and we cannot make excuses for it. We can't blame an addict's environment, or upbringing. Those things may contribute, but sin is a matter of choice. Despite popular perceptions, even casual drug use can have devastating consequences. Today's anti-drug messages

> Drugs weaken the mind's ability to think clearly, distinguish right from wrong, and exercise free will.

highlight some of them but tend to focus only on the physical effects of use. A young adult, who's committed his or her life to Christ, should know that drug use can damage his soul as well as his body.

"So then, let us not be like others, who are asleep, but let us be alert and self controlled. For those who sleep, sleep at night, and those who get drunk, get drunk at night. But since we belong to the day, let us be self-controlled, putting on faith and love as a breastplate, and hope of salvation as a helmet." – 1 Thessalonians 5:6-8 NIV.

You might know someone who has a drug problem. Don't write them off as gone yet. Help them. Pray for them. Love the sinner, but

> *Watch over your heart with all diligence. For from it flow the springs of life. – Proverbs 4:23 NASB.*

hate the sin. We must look beyond the sin to the sinner who has fallen victim to it. We must show love and kindness without excusing their sin, and offer help without condescending. Just be careful, you don't want to be dragged down into their sin.

As Christians we should abstain from art, music, or cinema that glorifies sin.

Jacob E. Wilcox

At least we should make a conscience effort to do so. Sometimes it's easier said than done.

One of the main reasons why God condemns intoxication is that as Christians we face many serious temptations. In order to distinguish right from wrong and then have the willpower to resist evil, our minds must think clearly so we may control our bodies. Self-control is one of the primary virtues of the Christian life. Christians are instructed to be in control of their decision making processes and not enslaved to anything that erodes their ability to act in ways that are honoring to God. A clear mind (which is impossible under the influence of drugs) is crucial to self-control. We should not please ourselves or other people in activities that tempt us to sin or that endanger our service to God.

A person who uses drugs generally starts because of peer pressure, which we've talked about, they give into temptation from others. The more involved they become, the greater the temptations become and the weaker the will to resist is. Alcohol and cigarettes are the first step towards marijuana use. To use them is to take drugs for pleasure, so why not move to greater "pleasure"? Friends encourage or pressure them, and so they try it. They enjoy the "high" and want it more often. Then they start having problems in school, on the job, or at home, so they take it more and more to escape reality.

Maybe the reason you are interested in drugs is that they seem to offer relief from pain. Maybe life isn't going the way you'd hoped. Maybe you've been abused. Maybe you've been rejected. Maybe your relationship has taken a turn for the worst. Maybe your parents divorced, and things are difficult, and you want relief.

> Drugs often lead to accidents or other dangerous or even violent behavior. Many people die or are seriously injured due to overdose. And many suffer torment from withdrawal.

But some methods of relief are better than others. God provides us a way to handle any temptation or problem in life. *"No Temptation has seized you except what is common to man. And God is faithful; he will not let you be tempted beyond what you can bear."* – *1 Corinthians 10:13 NIV.* You don't need to escape reality by means of drugs. You can avoid it and find your needs met in Jesus; let Him change your life. The Bible says your body is a temple for God who dwells in you, and it is not your own. Jesus Christ paid the highest price imaginable so you could live. Therefore you have to look after your body. Filling it with drugs or alcohol is not looking after it!

If you are not on drugs, great! Make sure you have the courage to refuse any attempt. There are no good stories about people who stay on illegal drugs.

A life of drugs is a life of despair, hopelessness, guilt, sorrow, and eventually death physically and eternally. Jesus is the real answer. His way is a way of life, hope, salvation, forgiveness, and eternal life.

"…He became the author of eternal salvation unto all them that obey him." – *Hebrews 5:9 KJV.*

Fifteen

Homosexuality/Transgender

Thou shalt not lie with mankind, as with woman kind; it is abomination. – Leviticus 18:22 KJV

If a man also lie with mankind, as he lieth with a woman, both of them have committed an abomination: they shall surely be put to death; their blood shall be upon them. – Leviticus 20:13 KJV

For this cause God gave them up unto vile affections: for even their women did change the natural use into that which is against nature. And likewise also the men, leaving the natural use of the women, burned in their lust one toward another; men with men working that which is unseemly, and receiving in themselves that recompence of their error which was meet. – Romans 1:26-27 KJV

Do you not know that the unrighteous will not inherit the kingdom of God? Do not be deceived. Neither fornicators, nor idolaters, nor adulterers, nor homosexuals, nor sodomites, nor thieves, nor covetous, nor drunkards, nor revilers, nor extortioners will inherit the kingdom of God. – 1 Corinthians 6:9-10 NKJV

Flee fornication. Every sin that a man doeth is without the body; but he that committeth fornication sinneth against his own body. – 1 Corinthians 6:18 KJV

"A woman shall not wear men's clothing, nor shall a man put on a woman's clothing; for whoever does these things is an abomination to the Lord your God. — Deuteronomy 22:5 NASB

The purpose for this chapter is to explain what God's never changing word says about homosexuality. It is not just my fallible opinion on this topic rather it is what God says in His Holy Word.

Homosexuality has become so common today, just as in the ancient pagan tribes, that it is considered an acceptable or even preferable lifestyle. God, however, who created men and women and ordained the proper and fruitful institution of marriage and the family unit, calls it abomination.

Despite modern theories, it is not a natural condition; it is a learned behavior which, like any other sin prohibited by a Holy God, can become a very difficult behavior to change when long practiced. Nevertheless, the Bible clearly forbids not only homosexuality, but also adultery, incest, bestiality, and any other type of sexual behavior except that in monogamous, lifelong marriage.

God can and does forgive these and other sins. Persistent and unrepentant sexual sin will eventually result in the judgment implicit in Romans 1:27, *"receiving in themselves that recompense of their error which was meet."* – (Morris, p. 219)

Homosexuality is a deadly trend that has gained popularity over the last few years. It is not only a deadly trend, but it is also a terrible sin. Homosexuality turns God's wonderful design for man and woman into something totally opposite. Satan likes to take God's words and plans and change them so that they are completely opposite of what He had originally planned. Take the rainbow for instance. It used to represent a beautiful promise that God would never

> Have you forgotten your Creator? Or are you taking the stand for Christ?

flood the Earth again, but now homosexuals are using it as the symbol for their movement!

Because of this movement many churches around the globe, have split and fallen into the "we must be tolerant" lifestyle. Many Christians who take a stand for Christ are labeled as "haters" or "intolerant" and are rejected by many. The tolerant become set in their ways and don't even want to hear the truth. However unbelief doesn't make it less true.

"Since they did not think it worthwhile to retain the knowledge of God, He gave them over to a depraved mind; to do what ought not to be done." – Romans 1:28 NIV.

"For this people's heart has become calloused; they hardly hear with their ears, and they have closed their eyes. Otherwise they might see with their eyes, hear with their ears, understand with their hearts and turn, and I would heal them." – Matthew 13:15 NIV.

These churches are accepting homosexuals' sinful state, and essentially saying homosexuality is not a sin. Now don't get me wrong; as a Christian we ought to love and accept everyone no matter what they've done. However we must not accept their sinful state. I've said it before and I'll say it again, "love the sinner hate the sin." That is how Christ wants us to approach this deadly trend along with any other trends.

If the church is divided on subjects like these, people won't be enthusiastic about becoming a Christian; we must unite together under our God to win souls.

How do I know that homosexuality is sinful? Well, for one the Bible says so many different times. In 1 Corinthians 6:9-10 NKJV it says: *"Do you not know that the unrighteous will not inherit the kingdom of God? Do not be deceived. Neither fornicators, nor idolaters, nor adulterers, nor homosexuals, nor sodomites, nor thieves, nor covetous, nor drunkards, nor revilers, nor extortioners will inherit the kingdom of God."*

Or you can look in Leviticus 18:22 KJV: *"Thou shalt not lie with mankind, as with woman kind; it is an abomination."* There are other scriptures in which I put in the beginning of this chapter.

It is also sinful because God did not design us that way. God made male and female. We are like puzzle pieces in God's big puzzle. There is only one piece that can fit into the other. It simply will not work any other way.

> *"All flesh is not the same flesh: but there is one kind of flesh of men, another flesh of beast, another of fishes, and another of birds." – 1 Corinthians 15:39. KJV*

Many people think that God exists to make all our dreams come true, and to give us unlimited pleasure. This perspective has influenced our society's view of the body. They think our bodies are blank slates in which we can make any identity we please; this is not so. The body is made by God for His glory. We were made to acknowledge and give the Lord glory. Our gender is not incidental; it has been given to us by our wonderful Savior as a gift.

Satan, hiding behind movements like feminism and the sexual revolution, has disrupted our culture and bended it to his will. Homosexuality is just another one of Satan's attempts to lure people from Christ. There is nothing more important in our culture than the art of manhood and womanhood. God designed us with specific tasks. A man is supposed to protect and preserve his family. The woman is supposed to teach and raise the family in a Godly prospective. Homosexuality completely changes that.

So what are we supposed to do as Christians? We must abandon the art of political correctness and stand up with strength and courage for Christ. We must deny Satan our culture, by working to change it through prayer. Our society is in desperate need of revival. We must launch an aggressive campaign of prayer, we must treat homosexuals like we treat all sinners, with love and a desire to change their spirit for Christ, only then will we see change.

Jacob E. Wilcox

To those who have embraced homosexuality, repentance is necessary and turning back to God is the only way you can be saved. We cannot live for God while embracing sin.

Questions

1. How can you minister the truth to homosexuals?

Sixteen

Pornography

You may say, "I am allowed to do anything." But I reply, "Not everything is good for you." And even though "I am allowed to do anything," I must not become a slave to anything. You say, "Food is for the stomach, and the stomach is for food." This is true, though someday God will do away with both of them. But our bodies were not made for sexual immorality. They were made for the Lord, and the Lord cares about our bodies. – 1 Corinthians 6:12 NLT

They don't care anymore about right or wrong, and they have given themselves over to immoral ways. Their lives are filled with all kinds of impurity and greed. – Ephesians 4:19 NLT

Flee from sexual immorality. All other sins a man commits are outside his body, but he who sins sexually sins against his own body. Do you not know that your body is a temple of the Holy Spirit, who is in you, whom you have received from God? You are not your own; you were bought at a price. Therefore honor God with your body. – 1 Corinthians 6: 18-20 NIV

Finally brothers, whatever is true, whatever is noble, whatever is right, whatever is pure, whatever is lovely, whatever is admirable – if anything is excellent or praiseworthy – think about such things. – Philippians 4:8 NIV

> *... I tell you that anyone who looks at a woman lustfully has already committed adultery with her in his heart. If your right eye causes you to sin, gorge it out and throw it away. It is better for you to lose one part of your body than for your whole body to be thrown into hell. And if your right hand causes you to sin, cut it off and throw it away. It is better for you to lose one part of your body than for your whole body to go into hell.*
> *– Matthew 5:28-30 NIV*

I challenge you to read this chapter even if you do not have this terrible addiction, this will be helpful to never start.

Pornography is very dangerous to not only the mental and spiritual state of your body but also the physical state as well.

Pornography is a drug; looking at pornography releases a chemical in the brain called dopamine. This chemical makes the person feel good.

Pornography is addicting; the more pornography you see, the more dopamine your brain needs to feel good. Pornography has changed the brain to only respond to abnormally high levels of dopamine. So normal everyday activities leave you feeling unsatisfied.

Over time your brain begins to associate pornography with pleasure. This act can lead to lack of interest in real people and relationship problems.

When you get addicted you start to lose your mental morals of what's pure and innocent and what's dirty and shameful.

Pornography decreases your appetite for real relationships and increases your appetite for more pornography.

As time progresses you start to shut out friends and/or family. You seek isolation, and then you start focusing almost all your brain power on the pleasure of pornography and not God's wonderful pleasures that He gives people who obey him. The pleasures of God are much better then these short term worldly pleasures. God's pleasure is satisfying and holy, while our pleasure is shameful and degrading.

If you are addicted to pornography then you must find any way possible to get out of this horrible addiction. I'd suggest you find someone like a pastor or counselor to talk with about it.

Pornography decreases your ability to experience "true love" and a lasting relationship like marriage. It makes you look at relationships/friendships in ungodly ways. It taints your mind; it "scars you for life." With pornography comes dishonor and disrespect for the opposite sex. You look at them for what they can give you. You become selfish, greedy, not understanding, violent, dirty, etc. Your relationship "highways" become twisted and out of order – you jump from boy/girl to boy/girl seeking out pleasure that you want so badly, and after each failed relationship you come out wanting more and more. It is an urge that cannot be satisfied. No matter how many times you try to fill the "cup" (void) you always seem to come up empty. There's nothing that can keep that "cup" full – or is there? God can fill that void and keep it full, if you only ask Him and let Him work in your life. Lay all your problems and struggles down at the cross; let them go. A lot of times we give our stuff to Him but we secretly still hold on to it. You need to give it up entirely and let God take care of it.

> Use whatever tactics it takes to stay pure.

Don't try to get rid of your addiction by yourself. If you do that you are going to lose. With God you will win. That void that you are trying to fill in your heart is where the Holy Spirit is supposed to reside. But since you are embracing evil, the Holy Spirit cannot reside there. And since the Holy Spirit cannot reside with sin, it leaves you with a void that you cannot fill. So please ask God to help you with your addiction, let Him come into the void and fill it permanently. Only Jesus is adequate to fill the deep cavern of your soul!

If you have just asked Him to come into your life then you have been spiritually electrified by God.

If you do not have this addiction then Great! Pray every day that you don't fall into this horrible sin. Remain pure, steadfast and strong. Keep the Holy Spirit with you so you won't have that void in your heart. Make the commitment to purity (which you will learn in the next chapter).

Questions:

1. How can you prevent the temptation of pornography?
2. What can you do to help others with this sin?

Seventeen

Premarital Sex

Don't you realize that your bodies are actually parts of Christ?
Should a man take his body, which belongs to Christ, and join it to
a prostitute? Never! And don't you know that if a man joins himself
to a prostitute, he becomes one body with her? For the Scripture say,
"The two are united into one." – 1 Corinthians 6:15-16 NLT

Here is a subject that is rarely addressed in detail at church. Premarital sex (sex outside of marriage) is a sin but where does the Bible say this? One spot where it says this is in God's Ten Commandments. "You shall not commit adultery." This is saying that we should not have sex with anyone other than our spouse. But why does God say this? Why doesn't He want us to enjoy what He has given us?

God created sex as a symbol of one's commitment to another in marriage. It's a very special act that proves your intimacy with your significant other.

When you have sex with someone, you become physically and anatomically one with them. In other words you are joined with them physically forever. *"For this reason a man will leave his father and mother and be united to his wife, and they will become one flesh." – Genesis 2:24 NIV.* But it's more than just physical oneness; it's a spiritual union that takes place between you and your partner to God. God planned for this exclusive experience of discovery and pleasure to happen within the intimacy of marriage.

What happens if your relationship is with a girl or boy friend that you have had intercourse with and broke up later on, then after a while you find someone else, and then you have sex with them? You are already physically and emotionally one with the other person and now you are becoming one with another person. This is not only dangerous to your soul but it is also dangerous to your physical well being which I will get to further in this chapter.

"Flee fornication every sin that a man doeth is without the body; but he that committeth fornication sinneth against his own body." – 1 Corinthians 6:18 KJV.

In biblical usage "fornication" can mean any sexual contact outside <u>monogamous</u> marriage. It thus includes not only premarital sex, but also adultery, homosexual acts, remarriage after un-biblical divorce, and sexual acts with animals, all of which are explicitly forbidden in the law as given through Moses (Leviticus 20:10-21). Christ expanded the prohibition against adultery to include even sexual lusting (Matthew 5:28). – (Morris, pp. 1,743) Jesus told us that if we even look at someone with lust in our heart, it's a sin. If we look at someone and fantasize about them later on then that's a complete sin. This is when controlling our eyes comes into play (which I will talk about later).

If you do not have premarital sex you will be emotionally and spiritually healthier. If we live for the world and seek to gratify our fleshly desire, then as the Bible says we cannot please God (Romans 8:8). And as we strengthen our fleshly desires, our relationship with God will be destroyed.

If we abstain from premarital sex we will be physically healthier. If we only have sex when married then we will be protected from the risk of catching a sexually transmitted disease. *"Run from sexual sin! No other sin so clearly affects the body as this one does. For sexual immorality is a sin against your own body. – 1 Corinthians 6:18 NLT.*

There are consequences with sex and in the case of premarital sex some of those consequences can be devastating like an unwanted pregnancy, STD's, abortion, broken relationships with family and friends; those are just a few outcomes when we choose sex outside of marriage. *"It is God's will that you should be sanctified: that you should avoid sexual immorality; that each of you should learn to control his own body in a way that is holy and honorable, not impassionate lust like the heathen, who do not know God." – 1 Thessalonians 4:3-5 NIV.*

If we choose to live a pure and Godly life free from the chains of premarital sex then we will be emotionally healthier and stable. When you have sex before marriage you will carry with you all the memories from past experiences forever. And when you finally do get married those memories, emotional scars, and unwanted mental images can hinder and even ruin the marriage. What was meant to be a wonderful design from God can turn into something degrading and sinful. *"Marriage should be honored by all, and the marriage bed kept pure, for God will judge the adulterer and all the sexually immoral." – Hebrews 13:4 NIV.*

Have you ever heard this verse: *"Love is patient, love is kind, it does not envy, it does not boast, it is not proud, it is not rude, it is not self seeking, it is not easily angered, and it keeps no record of wrongs. Love does not delight in evil but rejoices with the truth. It always hopes, always perseveres." – 1 Corinthians 13:4-5 NIV.* Let's just look at the first and second one "Love is patient."

[8]Those controlled by the sinful nature cannot please God. [13] For if you live according to the sinful nature, you will die; but if by the Spirit you put to death the misdeeds of the body, you will live. – Romans 8:8, 13 NIV

We can learn the sincerity of our partner's love by their willingness, or lack, to wait. If your significant other doesn't want to wait until after marriage to have sex then you need to determine if that person is the right person for you. "Love is kind." If you really love someone you need to respect their body and their decision to refrain from premarital sex.

God wants us to be examples to unbelievers and we can't do that when we are engaged in blatant sin. *"Be an example to all believers*

Jacob E. Wilcox

in what you say, in the way you live, in your love, your faith, and your purity," – 1 Timothy 4:12 NIV. In Matthew 5:13 Jesus compares His followers to "salt" and "light" when we represent Him in the world. When we no longer shine the light of Jesus, when we lose our example, we lose our "saltiness." We become spiritually flavorless and bland. We then in turn lose our ability to attract the world to Christ. Luke 14:34-35 says that salt without saltiness is worthless not even fit for the manure pile.

If you are engaging in premarital sex you are sinning right in God's face. If your partner wants to engage in sex, then consider this as a warning about their spiritual condition. If you want to engage in premarital sex, then consider this as a warning sign of your own spiritual condition.

How can we resist our sex drive?

"Thoughts lead to attitudes, attitudes become actions, actions develop into habits and habits form the real you." – Author unknown

So we know now that premarital sex is a sin but how do we keep it out of our lives? How do we control our sex drive? How can we regain our purity if it was lost? Sexual purity is essential for a Christian; it's one of the many things that separates us from the world.

This sub-chapter is going to be addressing what men can do to fight this. If you are a woman reader I would recommend skipping to the next chapter. In this 21st century it seems like everyone is trying sex. So how can we stand against the sexual waves that pound on us? Sexual purity starts with the eyes. Your eyes are

> To break through to the other side, you must start by cutting off the sensual images reaching your mind through your eyes. – (Arterburn, p. 152)

the doorway to your heart. Your intake will become your outtake if it persists for too long. Whatever you look at will get stuck in your

80

brain and produce an outtake so if you look at sexually depicted images on the internet or barely dressed women, those images will stay with you; they'll fuel your sex drive. To stop this fueling of our sex drives we must learn to "bounce our eyes." It takes lots of practice and at first it might not work, but you just have to keep trying it will happen eventually – you are creating a new habit.

There's something you should also know: It's not a sin to be attracted to a girl, attraction to girls is natural. This is what Fred has to say in the book *Every Young Man's Battle*, "... It's natural for you to find a girl's beauty tugging at your eyes for attention. The temptation, however, is to fulfill these desires and attractions in a wrong way and to go beyond a natural and normal outlook. That means viewing a girl more as an extremely interesting collection of body parts rather than as a precious child of God."

We shouldn't treat girls as objects; we should treat them as people with feelings, a soul, and a mind.

While you are working on bouncing the eyes you also need to start strengthening your guard around your brain. Why? To capture any sensual thoughts that might still be hiding deep within your brain. Remember you already have your intake you now must keep it from becoming your outtake in the form of fantasies.

"... *There must not be even a hint of sexual immortality or any kind of impurity...*" – *Ephesians 5:3*. Our lustful minds are impure. Our mind fantasizes over the tiniest sexual thought; that is why we must take our thoughts captive. "*Casting down imaginations, and every high thing that exalteth itself against the knowledge of God, and bringing into captivity every thought to the obedience of Christ.*" – *2 Corinthians 10:5 KJV*. Capture those lustful thoughts that are already behind your defensive wall. As your wall

> Once you travel down the freeway of premarital sex, you can't back up. If you want your purity back, then you'll have to exit that freeway entirely. – (Arterburn, p. 18)

gets stronger and your mental "police force" gets better at subduing your thoughts, there will be less sexual fantasy and it will become easier to bounce your eyes and control your roaming brain. It gets easier as you progress.

All you need to do to win the sexual lust battles is to say when they come, "I'm not thinking about that today." It's a constant effort, a daily commitment, to keep from the fantasy thoughts – at first. But just remember that your spiritual walls are just being put up. But you must know that your walls will fail sometimes but you must continue to fight. That's why you have your "police force" to round up those impure thoughts that have made it through. So you are free from sexual impurity.

This is a path that every male must take; to stay pure or to embrace sexual sin. We all have or will walk this path. There is no way to dodge it. Brothers, we are all on the same path together.

"Blessed are the pure in heart, for they will see God." – Matthew 5:8 NIV.

Part Three

BIBLE TALK

Eighteen

A Deeper Look Into The Ten Commandments

"And God spake all these words, saying, I am the lord thy God, which have brought thee out of the land of Egypt, out of the house of bondage."
– Exodus 20:1-2 KJV

"Not only did God speak these words; He also later wrote them down Himself... Thus if any part of the Bible should be taken literally, it should be these Ten Commandments... Note also that the commandments are grouped into two distinct categories. The first four commandments set forth the relationship of man to God (20:3-11), the last six commandments deal with man to man." – (Morris, p. 157)

The Ten Commandments are extremely important because they are God's laws that He set forth for us. Therefore we must obey them if we want to obey God. In this chapter I am going to talk about each commandment, what each means and how we are to obey them. So let's get started shall we?

1: *"Thou shalt have no other god's before me." – Exodus 20:3 KJV.*

This one's quite simple; God doesn't want you to worship other gods. (Like Buddha, Muhammad, etc.) He is a jealous God, therefore He wants your full-fledged worship or none of it – you cannot be lukewarm.

Jacob E. Wilcox

2: *"Thou shalt not make unto thee any graven image or any likeness of anything that is in heaven above, or that is in the earth beneath, or that is in the water under the earth. Thou shalt not bow down thyself to them, nor serve them: for I the Lord thy God am a jealous God's visiting the iniquity of the fathers upon the children unto the third and fourth generation of them that hate me; and shewing mercy unto the thousands of them that love me, and keep my commandments." – Exodus 20:1-6 KJV.*

God doesn't want you to make anything an idol. What's an idol? It's anything that you place at a higher greatness than God. An idol can be a movie star, a band, a person, it can be anything.

3: *"Thou shalt not take the name of the Lord thy God in vain; for the Lord will not hold him guiltless that taketh His name in vain." – Exodus 20:7 KJV.*

"It is significant that pagans never take the names of their 'Gods' in vain; this is a practice unique to apostate Christians or others whose belief is in a personal transcendent Creator. Our Creator is to be believed, worshiped and obeyed, not trivialized or blasphemed." – (Morris, p. 158)

4: *"Remember the Sabbath day, to keep it holy. Six days shalt thou labor, and do all thy work: But the seventh day is the Sabbath of the Lord thy God: in it thou shalt not do any work, thou, nor thy son, nor thy daughter, nor thy manservant, nor maidservant, nor thy cattle, nor thy stranger that is within thy gates: For in six days the Lord made heaven and earth, the sea, and all that in them is, and rested the seventh day: Wherefore the Lord blessed the Sabbath day, and hallowed it. – Exodus 20:8-11 KJV.*

"It is important to note the principle of one rest day following six days of work. The Hebrew word for 'Sabbath' does not mean 'Saturday' or 'seventh day;' it means 'rest' or 'intermission'." – *Henry Morris Study Bible* pg. 158.

God wants us to have a day of rest and worship. This Commandment is not only important spiritually but also mentally.

When you work seven days a week without resting for a day, you will get depressed, and have loads of stress.

5: *"Honor thy father and thy mother: that thy days may be long upon the land which the Lord thy God giveth thee." – Exodus 20:12 KJV.*

This law is quite self-explanatory; God wants us to respect and obey our parents, but to a certain extent. The "universal obedience law" (as I like to call it) states the order in who you obey: God first, family second, Nation third, then others. If your family wants you to do something that God doesn't approve of then you must obey God first and not do that stuff. If your nation tells you to do something that your parents and/or family doesn't approve of then you must obey your parents/family. Now if your family, nation, and others want you to do something that God disapproves of, then God therefore overrules them all.

6: *"You shall not murder" – Exodus 20:13 NASB.*

Killing and murder are two different concepts; killing is the act of taking someone or something's life for self-defense or for food, like killing a deer. Murder is the act of taking someone's life without the excuse of self-defense.

I believe that certain killing is not wrong. During war you are killing soldiers. The Israelites went to war many times in the Bible, and God helped them win many battles. So if killing was wrong then God led His chosen people into sin. No! This law applies to murders as in: abortionists, assassins, and your everyday killing on the news.

> "There is more to life than simply knowing about Jesus. Our lives must be transformed by His divine power that is deepened by a daily communion with the Father." – Steve Queen, 2016.

Like I said earlier this law does not apply to people who defended themselves. Think of it this way, if someone had a gun and was about to shoot you, but you also had a gun, wouldn't you shoot the person before he shoots you?

Although self-defense is okay, it is still not a good thing, and shouldn't be exploited. For instance, if a bully threatens you, you shouldn't take matters into your own hands. I would suggest you go back and read the chapter about bullying if you want to do something about the bully.

7: *"Thou shalt not commit adultery" – Exodus 20:14 KJV.*

Adultery is not only having sexual intercourse with someone that is not your wife/husband, but it is also considered adultery if you even look at someone with lust in your heart when you are married and/or in a relationship.

8: *"Thou shalt not steal." – Exodus 20:15 KJV.*

Well, I can't say much here except that stealing is stealing. If you take something from someone else without getting permission to do so, it would be stealing; even if you are planning to give it back.

9: *"Thou shalt not bear false witness against thy neighbor." – Exodus 20:16 KJV.*

In other words this is saying "don't lie." We are to be truthful as believers in Christ by not telling lies or spreading rumors.

The saddest thing I have heard from a Christian is them lying to a sinner and saying that they are Christians when clearly their lifestyles does not show it. It sickens my soul to hear a Christian tell a non-Christian that they are going to Heaven. *"Simply let your 'yes' be 'yes,' and your 'no,' 'no;' anything beyond this comes from the evil one. – Matthew 5:37 NIV.*

10: *"You shalt not covet your neighbor's house. You shalt not covet your neighbor's wife, or his manservant or maidservant, his ox or his donkey, or anything that belongs to your neighbor." – Exodus 20:17 NIV.*

Covet means "To wish enviously; to crave possession of that which belongs to someone else." – Webster's Pocket Dictionary.

When you covet something you are sinning and as Christians we shouldn't covet. We should be joyful and content for what we already possess. So don't go coveting your friend's new sports car or clothing. The grass is never greener on the other side.

I hope this gave you a deeper understanding for God's special Ten Commandments. Now put what you learned to good use. Obey God's laws and have faith that when you obey Him you will make Him pleased and proud.

Questions

1. Do you obey the Ten Commandments? Think about it? If not why?
2. Do you obey God? If not why?
3. What are ways we can obey God and His Laws?

Nineteen

Creation/Evolution

In the beginning God created the heavens and the earth.
– Genesis 1:1 NIV.

"In a very real sense, the Book of Genesis is the most important book in the world, for it is the foundation upon which all the other 65 books of God's written Word have been based. When Jesus Christ, after His resurrection, gave a key Bible study to His disciples on the way to Emmaus, He began with Genesis! *'Beginning at Moses and all the prophets, He expounded unto them in all the scriptures the things concerning himself.' – Luke 24:27 KJV.* We would do well to follow His example. If we want to understand the New Testament, we first need to understand Genesis. The New Testament contains at least 200 direct quotations or clear allusions to events described in Genesis – more than from any other book in the Old Testament.

"All the great doctrines of Christianity – sin, atonement, grace, redemption, faith, justification, salvation, and many others – are first encountered in Genesis. The greatest doctrine of all – the special creation of all things by the eternal, self-existent God – is revealed in the very first chapter of Genesis, the foundation of all foundations. It is hardly surprising therefore, that the greatest attacks on the Bible have been directed against the integrity and authority of Genesis. Since the only alternative to creation is evolution, these attacks are all ultimately based on evolutionism, the assumption that this complex universe can somehow be explained apart from the infinite creative power of God.

"The creation account in Genesis is supported by numerous other references throughout the Bible, and this is true for all the later events recorded in Genesis as well. To some degree, archaeological discoveries, as well as other ancient writings and traditions, also support these events, but the only infallibly correct record of creation and primeval history is the Book of Genesis. Its importance cannot be overestimated." – (Morris, p. 5)

The creation account of Genesis is the foundation of the salvation message. Why did Christ die and rise back to life? To conquer death by restoring the relationship we have lost because of the sin we let loose as recorded in Genesis. Why will God create a new Heaven and Earth someday? To fix the one we broke. The creation account of Genesis cannot be ignored, it cannot be altered, and we must teach it like we teach the rest of the Bible. We must teach how important the creation account of Genesis is because if we treat it like something to be changed to fit our new "scientific findings" it will lead to doubt of scriptures. *"All scripture is given by inspiration of God, and his profitable for doctrine, for reproof, for correction, for instruction in righteousness: That the man of God may be perfect, thoroughly furnished unto all good works."* – *1 Timothy 3:16-17 KJV.*

The entire Bible is God's Word and we need to take all of it seriously by teaching and believing what the Bible says about origins. If we allow people to insert other secular worldviews into the Bible with theories like Progressive creationism or the Gap theory, which alters the meaning of Genesis, we are teaching people that we don't have to take the Bible literally.

> *But if you do warn the wicked man to turn from his ways, and he does not do so, he will die for his sin, but you will have saved yourself.* – *Ezekiel 33:9 NIV*

Trying to believe in billions of years of Evolution and the Bible will cause contradictions that lead to doubts, which leads to abandonment on faith all together. Evolution is a dangerous worldview that contradicts the Bible, replaces God with man, and causes Christians and non-Christians to doubt God's Word. Molecules-to-man Evolution is fallible theory that has absolutely no proof that it ever happened. It is a lie that has been around for years, and it has never been dropped because no one wants to admit that there may be a Creator.

I want to talk about two worldviews: Creation (Genesis) and Evolution. Let's define our terms: Creation is the theory that every living creature was created by supernatural being about 6,000 years ago. God created the Earth, every basic kind of animal and plant and the two first human beings during a six-day period, as recorded in Genesis 1-2.

Day One: God created space, earth, time and light.
Day Two: God created the atmosphere.
Day Three: God created dry land and plants.
Day Four: God created the sun, moon and stars.
Day Five: God created the sea creatures and birds of the air.
Day Six: God created the land animals and man.

This model of history is based on the Bible, God's perfect Word.

The other model of history, Evolution, states that all the animal species on Earth today all came about by billions upon millions of years of mutations and variations. They say that around 14 billion years ago the universe suddenly exploded into existence without any explanation. (There was nothing, and it blew up!) Then about three billion years ago the first living creature emerged from the oceans from a puddle of pre-biotic soup. (That's right, your ancestors were soup! Remember that next time you are at the grocery store!) After many generations this life form evolved into a fish, then to an amphibian, then into a reptile, then into a bird, then into mammal, and finally man. This type of transition from molecules to man is called Macroevolution, and it is unscientific and has not ever been proven. This theory of Earth history leaves a lot of unanswered questions, like how did the first lifeform come from non-living chemicals? Or how did this creature learn to reproduce itself? How did this creature learn to evolve? Eat? Breathe? Move? And the list keeps on going.

Creationists, however, have a book that tells us the answer to Earth history. "In the beginning, God created the heavens and the earth…" Evolutionists do not know where all the planets came from, so which do you believe, "<u>In the beginning…God,</u>" or <u>"In the beginning… nothing?"</u>

Theistic Evolution

Evolution and theistic evolution are completely different. One says there needs to be a higher being, a Creator; another says there is no need for a Creator, the universe made itself. So you either believe there is a Creator, or there isn't? Or perhaps you believe that the Creator created this world with evolution to govern its outcome, theistic evolution.

If you are going to say that God used the big bang and millions of years of molecules-to-man/evolution to create the animals and human beings, then I am going to say that's ridiculous. If you are a theistic evolutionist then you must believe that God used millions of years of evolution, death, bloodshed, pain, suffering and survival to finally get Man, His perfect creation?

When an animal develops a new characteristic that makes it better fit to survive, the rest have to die out to leave the one to produce offspring more fit to survive; that is how evolution is supposed to work. So this process had to have been going on for millions of years from the moment God created the Earth until millions of years after when you get to Adam and Eve who were living in a perfect world built on the bones of dead animals that had to die in order to allow the apes to evolve into us! That is not a perfect world!

So in essence, you think that God created this world with death and sin already present. Well, if that is true, then that means humans never ruined this world. That also means God is an evil God who created us to die. That means there was no reason for Jesus to come down to die and rise back to life. He did it to defeat death, but why defeat something He created as the natural process in nature? If you contradict the Creation account as recorded in Genesis, you've destroyed the entire foundation of the Bible!

Twenty

The Flood, Fact or Fiction

"And God looked upon the earth, and behold, it was corrupt; for all flesh had corrupted his way upon the earth. [13]. And God said unto Noah, the end of all flesh is come before me; for the earth is filled with violence through them; and behold, I will destroy them with the earth. [14]. Make thee an altar of gopher wood; rooms... [15]. ...The length of the ark shall be three hundred cubits (450ft), the breadth (width) of it fifty cubits, (75ft) and the height of it thirty cubits (45ft). [16.] Make a roof for it. Leave the sides the sides of the ark open a foot and a half from the top. Put a door in one side of the ark. Make lower, middle and upper decks. [17] And behold I will bring flood of waters upon the earth, to destroy all flesh, wherein is the breath of life, from under heaven; and everything that is in the earth shall die. [18]. But with thee will I establish my covenant; and thou shalt come into the ark, thou, and thy sons, and thy wife, and thy sons wives with thee. [19] And of every living thing of all flesh, two of every sort shalt thou bring into the ark, to keep them alive with thee; they shall be male and female. [20]. Of fowls after their _kind, of every creeping thing of the earth _after his kind_, two of every sort shall come unto thee, to keep them alive._

[7:4]. for yet seven days, and I will cause it to rain upon the earth forty days and forty nights; and every living substance that I have made will I destroy from off the face of the earth. [5]. And Noah did according unto all that the lord commanded him. [11]. In the six hundred year of Noah's life, in the second month, the

seventeenth day of the month, the same day were all the fountains of the great deep broken up, and the windows of heaven were opened. [12[And the rain was upon the earth forty days and forty nights. [18]. and the waters prevailed, and were increased greatly upon the earth, and the ark went upon the face of the waters. [19]. And the waters prevailed exceedingly upon the earth; and all the high hills, that were under the whole heaven, were covered. [21]. and all flesh died that moved upon the earth, both of fowl, and of cattle, and of beast, and of every creeping thing that creepeth upon the earth, and every man: [22]. All in whose nostrils was the breath of life, of all that was in the dry land, died. [24]. and the waters prevailed upon the earth an hundred and fifty days."
– Genesis 6:12-20; 7:4, 5, 11,12,18,19,21,22,24 KJV.

A lot of people dismiss the flood, or believe it's just a myth. But, the flood was a big part of Earth's history, and a real worldwide catastrophic event that changed the world into something very different than before! I'll talk about that later, right now I want to talk about the "famous" Ark. Some people paint a picture of the ark in their mind as a little tiny ship with barely enough room for Noah and his family let alone animals. But that's not what the boat was; it was a large vessel capable of carrying all the animals including Noah and his family. *"…The length of the ark shall be three hundred cubits (450ft), the breadth (width) of it fifty cubits, (75ft) and the height of it thirty cubits (45ft). A window shalt thou make to the ark, and in a cubit shalt thou finish it above; and the door of the ark shalt thou set in the side thereof; with lower, second, and third stories shalt thou make it." – Genesis 6:15-16 KJV.* According to this scripture, the ark was gigantic; the dimensions of the ark were ideal for stability and capacity. The ark would have been nearly impossible to capsize.

A lot of skeptics ask the question how did Noah fit all the different species of animals into the ark? There are thousands of different kinds species? *"Of fowls after their <u>kind</u>, and of cattle after their <u>kinds</u>, of every creeping thing of the earth after his <u>kind</u>..."* – Genesis 6:20 KJV. The Bible uses the word "kinds" not species. Yes there are thousands of species, for instance, look at a dog. There are many species of dogs but if you just trace them back to their "ancestor" it was a dog. Noah didn't need to bring all the different variations of dogs; he only brought the kind needed to reproduce, so all the dogs today are just variations of the two dogs on the ark.

Many atheists ask the question, "Where did all that water come from"?

In the pre-flood world there wasn't much visible water. (I will go into more depth in the sub-chapter.) *"... On that day all the springs of the great deep burst forth, and the floodgates of the heavens were opened."* – Genesis 7:1 NIV. Henry Morris gives a good description of what happened and where the water came from in his Study Bible: "The physical cause of the flood is clearly identified as the eruption of waters in the "Great deep" and the opening of the floodgates of Heaven. These are quite sufficient in themselves to cause and explain all the phenomena of the flood. The pre-flood water cycle was apparently controlled by a system of subterranean pressurized reservoirs and conduits, but these fountains were all cleaved open in one day releasing tremendous quantities of water and magma to the Earth's surface and dust and gas into the atmosphere. The resulting combination of atmospheric turbulence and dust was probably of the primeval deep. The result left the pre-flood world completely devastated and inundated." – (Morris, p. 37)

But not all the water came from the ground, before the flood there was a vapor canopy in the highest parts of the atmosphere. (Which I will talk about later.)

The vapor canopy surrounded the Earth and created a perfect environment on Earth. When the flood came God forced the water down to the Earth. That caused it to rain for forty days and nights. *"And rain was upon the earth forty days and forty nights."* – Genesis 7:12 KJV. Henry Morris says it well in his Study

Bible: "Not only would all the land animals eventually drown, but the plant covering would be uprooted and rafted away, the soils eroded and finally even the mountains and hills washed away. In the sea depths, the eruption of fountains of the great deep would also profoundly affect marine life. Great quantities of magma, metals and other materials were extruded from the earth's mantle. The sediments from the lands were transported down to be deposited in the encroaching sea basins complex hydrodynamic phenomena-tsunamis, vortices, turbidity flows, cyclic erosion and deposition, and a variety of geomorphic activity took place throughout the year.

"Earth movements of great magnitude, and tremendous volcanic explosions shook the earth again and again, until finally, the world that then was being overflowed with water perished." – (Morris, p. 37).

Pre-Flood World

Now the pre-flood world was very different from our nowadays world. Before the flood there was an "ice" or "vapor" canopy surrounding the Earth (which I will discuss more later on). With this canopy in the heavens, it kept out harmful sunlight, and made the Earth like a "greenhouse" allowing the planet to be lush and green. Also before the flood there were no natural pollutants like volcanoes. The oxygen therefore was pure, allowing plants to grow at excessive rates. With the harmful rays of the sun gone and pure oxygen plentyful, close decendents of Adam would live longer and grow larger. Before the flood people would live to be 900. Adam lived to be 930, Methuselah was the oldest, living to 969. Noah lived to be 950.

> The reason for longevity is because of the close relationship to Adam. There weren't much genetic mutations because Adam was made perfect without the genetic mutations.

Someone can't really live to be 900, can they? Studies show that due to constant production of new cells replacing old ones, the body is surprisingly self-sustaining, and with the right atmospheric conditions your body might as well be immortal.

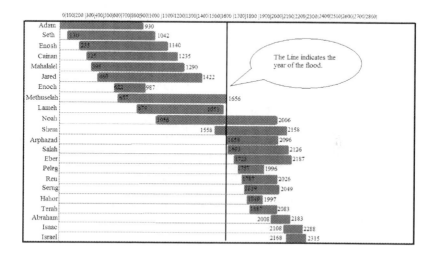

The Line indicates the year of the flood.

OK, so living to be 900, that's a long time. How much information could you obtain in a span of 900 years? A lot! You could pursue multiple careers like science, music, politics, etc. Calculating all the ages, you can see that Adam could have known Noah's dad, and Adam walked with God.

Do you know how much knowledge and wisdom Adam could have obtained and shared straight from God? The pre-flood flood world could have been ripe with new technologies and inventions that we would never even imagine. Evolutionists and other secular people have gotten the wrong idea of our past, they believe we were dumb and are getting smarter and smarter, but really we were smart to begin with.

There were creations back then that we can't copy today. Don Landis says it well in his book "According to Genesis 4, the pre-flood civilization had farms, livestock, music, cities, and tools, yet it is impossible to say how much technology they possessed. One would

Jacob E. Wilcox

speculate that they had abilities due to their close descent from Adam and Eve, the most intelligent humans created. Furthermore, this seemingly short section of the Bible encompasses over 1,500 years of civilization, giving early man generations to learn and advance. Often times, people do not fully comprehend the length of time between creation and the flood. Just think, the radio was invented in the late 1800s and in only a little over 200 years, technology has advanced to include automobiles, space shuttles, cellular phones, and the internet. It would be foolish to assume that over 1,500 years these people were unable to advance any further than Tubal-Cain's bronze and iron forgery." – (Landis, p. 43)

Some people just brush the ages aside but you need to know how important it is. What if Sir Isaac Newton lived long enough to finish his theory of physics, or lived to work with Albert Einstein? What would they have come up with? You see the ages are very important, you can't just discard them, you must accept them.

> "Zil-lah also had a son, Tubal-Cain, who forged all kinds of tools out of bronze and iron..." – Genesis 4:22 NIV

The Canopy Theory

The canopy theory: The theory that before the flood, there was a layer of water above the atmosphere.

"And God said, let there be a firmament in the midst of the water, and let it divide the waters from the waters. And God made the firmament, and divided the waters which were under the firmament from the waters which were above the firmament: and it was so. And God call the firmament heaven..." – Genesis 1:6-8a NKJV.

This firmament split the water in two: the water on the earth (oceans, lakes, and streams) from the water over our atmosphere (vapor or frozen layer).

Why This Firmament Is Not In Space

"And God said, 'let the waters under the heaven be gathered together into one place, and let dry land appear'; and it was so." – Genesis 1:9 NKJV.
This indicates that the water on the surface of the earth formed oceans. If Heaven was space, they would not use the term, "under heaven."
"…And fowl that may fly above the earth in the open firmament of heaven." – Genesis 1:20 KJV. Birds don't fly in space; they fly in the atmosphere, the sky, the firmament.

Problems With The Canopy Theory

"And God said, let there be lights in the firmament of heaven to divide the day from night; and let them be for signs and season, and for days; and years: And let them be for lights in the firmament of the heaven to give light upon the earth; and it was so." – Genesis 1:14-15 KJV.
This and another verse shows that God put stars and sun and moon in the firmament, but how could they fit in our atmosphere? Sun, moon and stars are in space. So is the firmament or "heaven" space, not the atmosphere that splits the water? This can't be, we have already discovered that birds fly in this firmament, they can't fly in space. This has led to many doubts. Was the firmament the atmosphere or space?

A Second Firmament

Here are the facts: God split the water, one formed oceans on the earth, and the other went up, and in between these two bodies of water was a space, firmament or heaven. Some think this second layer of water surrounded the earth and formed a water canopy which was composed of water vapor or frozen barrier, thus the firmament is the sky. Others think it went all the way past our galaxy, and formed a barrier enclosing the universe in water; thus the firmament is space. But the controversy comes from the fact that the Bible says that God put the sun, moon, and stars in the firmament of heaven which can't be the atmosphere. So could there be more than one firmament?

The word *heaven* in the Hebrew is plural (like our word for moose, and deer); so Heaven could actually mean *heavens* (which is how it is translated in the NIV Bible). So what if space was called Heaven and the atmosphere was called heaven; and firmament is translated as "sky" or "space," the space between. So the sky and space could both be called spaces between. So if we believe that both the sky and space was called the "firmament of Heaven," then we can conclude that there was a water canopy, and a firmament that separated them.

So in conclusion; God created the sky to separate the water canopy from the oceans; this firmament is what we are in right now, Heaven, one of three heavens. Space is also called Heaven. The water canopy fell down during the flood; losing God's pre-flood world. I get these conclusions from the Bible, God's Holy Word.

Twenty-one

Prophecies In The Bible

Unique among every book written or that will be written, the Holy Bible accurately foretells specific events in detail many years, sometimes centuries, before they happen. About 2,500 prophecies appear in the Bible and about 2,000 of them have already been fulfilled to the letter – no errors. The other 500 go into the future and could be unfolding as you are reading through this book.

Satan (being the evil person he is) is trying to conceal these prophecies from you. Satan knows the Bible and its prophecies. He is fully aware that the truth is the strongest weapon to use against him and his lies. That is why he is doing everything he can to keep us "entertained" so that we cannot see what is right in front of us.

When we seek the truth and live according to it, Satan's lies and deceptions become utterly useless, because we are under the Holy Spirit, which Satan cannot penetrate. This is why we must seek out the truth. However, we shouldn't focus too much attention on end-time signs. It will distract us from our goal that we are on Earth for, and that's spreading the gospel and ministering to people about Jesus. That's what we as Christians need to be doing.

Oh and by the way, Jesus said in Matthew 24:36, *"But of that day and hour knoweth no man, no, not the angels of heaven, but my father only."* So therefore it is impossible to know the day and hour of our Lord's return. So how do we prepare for the end-times? The Bible says that we must remain vigilant and ready spiritually, not physically. We also need to get as many people as we can to Jesus, that is our calling, that's all we can do. So go and minister to people! Write a book like I did, sing songs, talk to people, etc. Do something for Jesus because the rapture can happen at any moment; it will happen if you're ready or not. *"For you know very well that the day of the Lord will come like a thief in the night." – 1 Thessalonians 5:2 NIV*

Twenty-two

The Great Spoiler

*Spoiler Alert: This content contains spoilers
of the Bible and its teachings!*

Isn't a spoiler the worst? Especially when you are looking forward to the thing that was spoiled, like a new movie, book, or play. We get the worst feeling when someone who has already seen it says something that will just ruin the whole thing (at least I do). The world's spoilers are the worst, but God's spoilers are the best. You're probably thinking "Jacob, where and when did God release spoilers?"

If you are a Christian, then God has already told you what happens at the end. He told you what will happen when you take that last breath, when you say that last word. You will be with Him in Heaven.

That's a major spoiler! He not only spoiled our personal ending of our lives, but He also spoiled the ending to everything in life.

If you just take a look at Revelation and other books of the Bible you will know how it will all play out. (There is so much spoiling going on in Revelation that they should change the name "Revelation" to "The Great Big Spoiler.")

The ending of God's story has been written in the very last pages of the Bible. *"Then I saw a new heaven and a new earth, for the first heaven and the first earth had passed away, and there was no longer any sea. I saw the Holy City, the New Jerusalem, coming down out of heaven from God, prepared as a bride beautifully dressed for her husband. And I heard a loud voice from the throne saying. 'Now the dwelling of God is with men, and He will live with them, they will be His people, and God himself will be with them and be their God. He will wipe every tear from their eyes. There will be no more death or mourning or crying or pain, for the old order of things has passed away.' He who was seated on the throne said, 'I am making everything new!' Then He said, 'Write this down, for these words are trustworthy and true.' He said to me: 'It is done. I am the Alpha and the Omega, the Beginning and the End. To him who is thirsty I will give to drink without cost from the spring of the water of life. He who overcomes will inherit all this, and I will be his God and he will be my son. But the cowardly, the unbelieving, the vile, the murderers, the sexually immoral, those who practice magic arts, the idolaters and all liars – their place will be in the fiery lake of burning sulfur. This is the second death." – Revelation 21:1-8 NIV.*

God's going to end this terrible sin stained earth and heaven (universe) and make a new Heaven and Earth that is without sin. It's going to be great! We would be living in the direct presence of God. Imagine sitting on God's lap having a conversation with Him!

> *To him who overcomes and does my will to the end, I will give authority over the nations. – Revelation 2:26 NIV*

This new Earth will be without sin's curse therefore there will be:

No more pain (especially if you stub your toe, praise Jesus for that!)
No more lying or secrets.
No more fear.
No more sorrow.
No more sinful thoughts to cloud your mind.
No more jealousy.
No more bullies.
All evil will be gone for good; there will be no trace of sin.
"They will never again be hungry or thirsty, and they will be fully protected from the scorching noontime heat." – Revelation 7:16 NLT.

All of God's "Children" will be given a brand spankin' new body; a real body.

We won't be just spirits floating around in the clouds. Our bodies will not be affected by sin's curse; they will be perfect. We will run and not grow weary and we will walk for miles and not faint. Our bodies will be in the perfect health and shape. We all will be content with our bodies.

It will be like this Earth but "unexplored." As we journey around and explore, we will praise our infinite Creator. There will be new mountains to climb, new songs to sing, new pictures to paint. As we do all these wonderful things our joy will increase daily and we will flourish.

A decent amount of people think the new Heaven and Earth will be just like a non-stop church service, but it's going to be much more. Your life will be more real than the reality of today. We will certainly be praising our Lord but we will be doing other daily life activities too, just in the direct presence of God.

So I just gave you a couple of spoilers, but I saved the best spoiler for last.

Spoiler Alert: Jesus wins.

No matter what happens here on Earth Jesus is going to win, the end is going to be what God has spoken. So be prepared for Him to call His believers to Him.

Be faithful and don't forget that God spoiled the ending for us. God has broken the record for the most insane spoiler in history.

Behold, I am coming soon! Blessed is he who keeps the words of the prophecy in this book. – Revelation 22:7 NIV

Twenty-three

The Evil That Stains Our World

If God loves us, then why is there evil and suffering? Why would a God that loves us make us suffer?

The answer is simple. God gave us a free will to follow Him or to disobey Him. This however does not answer all concerns (because He sometimes does intervene in world situations), but suggests that the problem of evil is not as great an intellectual obstacle to belief as some imagine. Look at the soil for a moment. It naturally produces weeds. Nobody plants them. Nobody waters them. They even push through cracks of a sidewalk and roadways. Millions of weeds sprout everywhere, strangling our crops and ruining our lawns.

Look at how much of the Earth is uninhabitable. There are millions upon millions of square miles of nothing but barren deserts in Africa and in different parts of the world. Most of Australia is desert. There is nothing but miles and miles of useless desolate land.

The earth is constantly rocked by earthquakes. Its shores are beaten with hurricanes, tornadoes tear through the countryside. Floods soak the land, and terrible droughts parch the ground. Sharks, tigers, lions, snakes, spiders and disease-ridden mosquitoes attack humanity and suck its life giving blood. The Earth's inhabitants are afflicted with disease, pain and death.

Think of how many people are plagued with cancer, heart disease, and a many other diseases. Think of all the kids with leukemia, or people born with crippling diseases or without the mental capability to even feed themselves.

What's wrong with this world? Did God blow it when He created humanity? What sort of tyrant must our Creator be if this was His master plan?

Sadly, many people use this issue as an excuse to reject any thought of a divine Savior, when its existence is the very reason we should accept Him. Suffering stands as a terrible testimony to the truth of the explanation given by the Word of God. It is the supernatural testament of our Creator as to why there is suffering and what we can do about it.

The Bible tells us that God cursed the Earth because of Adam and Eve's sin. Disease, sin, and suffering are curses; the Scriptures inform us that we live in a fallen world.

> Man was created to be dependent on God, but suddenly became independent from God.

In the beginning, God created man perfect and he lived in a perfect world, without suffering (it was Heaven on Earth). When sin came into the world, death came with it.

Those who understand the teachings of the Scripture eagerly await a new Heaven and a new Earth "wherein dwells righteousness." In that coming Kingdom there will be no more pain, no more suffering, no disease and no death.

We are told in 1 Corinthians 2:9 that no eye has ever seen, nor has any ear heard, neither has any man's mind ever imagined the wonderful things that God has in store for those that love Him.

Think for a moment of what it would be like if food grew like weeds. Think how wonderful it would be if the deserts became fertile, if creation stopped devouring humanity. Imagine if disease disappeared, if pain was gone, if death was no more.

There is an adage that says, "If it sounds too good to be true, it probably is." That is solid advice for when you are dealing with sinful mankind. But the promise of a new Heaven and a new Earth come from a faithful Creator, and there is no greater insult to God than not to believe His promises.

The dilemma is that we are like a small child whose insatiable appetite for candy has caused his face to break out. He looks in the mirror and he sees a sight that makes him very depressed. His face is nothing but ugly and sickening sores. But instead of stopping eating his candy, he takes joy in stuffing more into his mouth. Yet, his very joy is actually the cause of his suffering.

The whole face of the Earth is nothing but ugly sores of suffering. Everywhere we look, we see unbearable pain. But instead of believing God's explanation and asking Him to forgive us and change our appetite, we run deeper into sin's sweet embrace. There we find happiness in its <u>temporary</u> pleasures – thus intensifying our pain, both in this life, and in the life to come.

But it's not going to be like this forever. Yes, the Earth is going to die; it is a non-renewable resource. But there is a place that, as Christians, we can look forward to, and that's Heaven.

Twenty-four

"Heaven"

Be not rash with thy mouth, and let not thine heart be hasty to utter anything before God: for God is in heaven, and thou upon the earth: therefore let thy words be few. – Ecclesiastes 5:2 KJV

For we know that if our earthly house of this tabernacle were dissolved, we have a building of God, and house not made with hand, eternal in the heavens. – 2 Corinthians 5:1 KJV

…Well done, good and faithful servant! You have been faithful with a few things; I will put you in charge of many things. Come and share your master's happiness! – Matthew 25:23 NIV

Jesus describes the kingdom of Heaven in Matthew 13, using parables and mental illustrations. I encourage you to read the chapter, but since it is really long I won't "torture" you by putting it in this book.

> *"… Eye hath not seen, nor ear heard, neither have entered into the heart of man, the things which God hath prepared for them that love him." – 1 Corinthians 2:9 KJV*

Paul wrote in Romans 14:17 *"for the kingdom of God is not meat and drink; but righteousness and peace and joy in the Holy Ghost."* What he's saying is that Heaven isn't <u>just</u> all things pleasurable to you, but is more spiritual than material. He also says in

1 Corinthians 2:9 *"… Eye hath not seen, nor ear heard, neither have entered into the heart of man, the things which God hath prepared for them that love him."* The glories of Heaven are beyond human imagination, for they are being prepared for us by Christ himself. When Apostle Paul was stoned in Lystra, he died, and was taken up to Heaven and then came back. He saw beautiful things in Heaven, but was forbidden to reveal them to us.

"… He was caught up into paradise, and heard unspeakable words, which it is not lawful for a man to utter." – 2 Corinthians 12:4 KJV. Now the words that Paul heard in Heaven weren't curse words, they were words that cannot be communicated to mortal ears. "Perhaps certain aspects of them, however, were given to enable him to convey the glorious promises of the future resurrection day (1 Corinthians 15:51-57; 1 Thessalonians 4:13-18). However, there were others which he was not allowed to communicate, even if he could." – (Morris, pp. 1,785)

So Heaven is unimaginable. You cannot comprehend the ways of God, or His dwelling place. If you could comprehend and understand everything that God is doing then God is not worthy to be worshiped. He is worshiped because He is outside of our intellect and imagination.

Heaven is an amazing place where – if you gave your heart to Him and seek His will daily – you will be when you die. God has some pretty cool stuff awaiting us up there in Heaven. *"In my father's house are many mansions: if it were not so, I would have told you. I go to prepare a place for you." – John 14:2 KJV.*

> *"And God shall wipe away all tears from their eyes; and*
> *there shall be no more death, neither sorrow, nor crying,*
> *neither shall there be any more pain: for the former*
> *things are passed away." – Revelation 21:4 KJV*

"Thy Kingdom is an everlasting kingdom, and thy dominion endureth throughout all generations." – Psalms 145:13 KJV

Questions

1. If you look at your life right now, will you go to Heaven?
2. How can you teach about Heaven to people?

Twenty-five

"Hell"

*And these will go away into eternal punishment, but the
righteous into eternal life. – Matthew 25:46 KJV*

*And I (John) saw the dead, great and small, standing before the
throne, and the books were opened. Then another was opened, which
is the book of life. And the dead were judged by what was written in
the books, according to what they had done. – Revelation 20:12 KJV*

*So it will be at the close of the age. The angels will come
out and separate the evil from the righteous and throw
them into the lake of fire. In that place will be weeping
and gnashing of teeth. – Matthew 13:49-50 KJV*

*Then said the king to the servants, "bind him hand and foot,
and take him away, and cast him into outer darkness; there shall
be weeping and gnashing of teeth." – Matthew 22:13 KJV*

*Raging waves of the sea, foaming out their own shame; wandering
stars, to whom is reserved the blackness of darkness forever."
– Jude 13 KJV*

*For God sent not his son into the world to condemn the world, but
that the world through him might be saved. – John 3:17 KJV*

114

*And he cried and said, Father Abraham, have mercy on me, and
send Lazarus that he may dip the tip of his finger in water, and cool
my tongue; for I am tormented in this flame. – Luke 16:24 KJV*

Before I start talking about this topic I want to clarify that I am
not trying to scare you to believe in God. I am just trying to show
you that Hell is a real place – not the mystical unknown. Sometimes
we need a spiritual jump start back into the faith. Many of pastors
avoid preaching on Hell because they are very afraid people will stop
coming to their church or think that they are trying to scare them
into the faith.

Many Christians believe that there is no Hell; that God is just
love, and He wouldn't send His creation to the fiery damnation of
Hell. But Hell is real! Some people think Hell is just a place where it's
all fuzzy and hazy or just a word to scare people. But Hell is a very
clear and real place, where you can feel, hear, taste, etc. What I want
to address in this chapter is "the unknown hell." There is currently
a big battle going on for your soul. It has been going on since the
day you were born. There is a special world around us, but we can't
see it because it is covered by a "spiritual veil." Behind this veil are
God's angels, the fallen angels, devils and spirits that harass us by
filling our brains with terrible thoughts to keep us from knowing
God and His words. They are out to get our souls!

When you die your soul will go to one of two places: one is
Heaven and the other Hell. Once you die in your sins, your soul
will go down to Hell, and what will you see and feel there? As your
soul falls down into Hell instantly you will sense terror more horrible
than you can think of. Imagine an active volcano and the smell of
sulphur (smells like rotten eggs). The soul cannot burn up because it
is not a physical body. But you can still feel, remember, and hear. In
Hell you can hear weeping, gnashing of teeth, screams of horror and
curses, but you'll see nothing (darkness). You will be utterly alone.

Could anything be worse? Yes…. the lake of fire is next. *"And death and hell were cast into the lake of fire. This is the second death. And whosoever was not found written in book of life was cast into the lake of fire." – Revelation 20:14-15 KJV.*

All those who are in Hell will be cast into something far worse. This is where they will burn for eternity. You can choose not to believe it, that's your choice but <u>unbelief will not put out the flames.</u> And yes, God does love us; He is our Father, and like any good Father He is going to correct His children if they have done something wrong. He corrects us because He loves us.

Some people say "I don't mind going to Hell. All my friends will be there." Those who say that don't believe in the biblical concept of Hell. This is simply because their understanding of the nature of God is erroneous. The slow-witted criminal thinks that the electric chair is a place to put up his feet for awhile and relax. It may be wise therefore to speak with him for a few minutes about the reasonableness of a place called Hell.

If a judge in Ohio turns a blind eye to the unlawful dealings of the Mafia; if he sees their murderous acts and deliberately turns the other way, is he a good or bad judge? He's obviously corrupt, and should be brought to justice himself. If he is a good judge, he will do everything within his power to bring those murderers to justice. He should make sure that they are justly punished.

If Almighty God sees a man rape and strangle your sister or mother to death, do you think He should look the other way, or bring that murderer to justice himself? It makes sense then that if God is good, He will therefore do everything in His power to make sure that justice is done. The Bible tells us that He will punish murderers; and the place of punishment where God will send them is called Hell. God should punish murderers and rapists. However, God is so good, He will also punish thieves, liars, adulterers, fornicators, and blasphemers, etc. He will punish those who desired to murder and rape but never had the opportunity. He warns that if we hate someone, we commit murder in our hearts. If we lust, we commit adultery in the heart, etc.

So what's your choice Heaven or Hell? I hope by the end of this book you will have made the right decision, but I want you to know that God/Christianity is not just fire insurance; being a Christian is about exploring the friendship and relationship you are supposed to have with God. You are in a covenant with Him once you are saved. God treats the relationship you have with Him like a marriage, so treat it like a marriage covenant: for better or worse, for richer or poorer, for sickness or health.

...Believe in the Lord Jesus Christ, and thou shalt be saved...
– Acts 16:31KJV.

Questions

1. Do you believe in Hell?
2. How can you teach about Hell?
3. If you look at your life right now, Where will you spend eternity?

Twenty-six

Investigating Satan

He will be a master of deception, defeating many by catching them off guard. Without warning he will destroy them. He will even take on the prince of princes in battle, but he will be broken, though not by human power. – Daniel 8:25 NLT

How you have fallen from heaven, O morning star, son of the dawn! You have been cast down to the earth, you who once laid low the nations! You said in your heart, 'I will ascend to heaven; I will raise my throne above the stars of God; I will sit enthroned on the mount of assembly, on the uttermost heights of the sacred mountain. I will ascend above the tops of the clouds; I will make myself like the Most High.' But you are brought down to the grave, to the depths of the pit. Those who see you stare at you, they ponder your fate: 'Is this the man who shook the earth and made kingdoms tremble, the man who made the world a desert, who overthrew its cities and would not let his captives go home?' – Isaiah 14:12-17 NIV

So we have been talking about temptation, sin, pain, depression, but we haven't really talked about the one who brings all that upon you.

The father of lies, angel of darkness, Lucifer, Satan, the devil; those are just a few names that he goes by. So who is he? What is his origin? Why would God

> The Devil has only the power that you give him.

create him? We all love origin stories so let's just start with his origin story.

The Bible says that Satan was created by God as a cherub which is the highest of the angels. Satan (his original name was Lucifer) was created as a perfect being; perfect in looks and brains, however Satan became prideful ("Your heart was lifted up because of your beauty"). He decided to take the throne and rule the universe himself. At that point rebellion started in Heaven; Satan convinced one-third of the angels to join him in his rebellion against God.

Michael, an archangel of God, fought with God's angels against Lucifer and his angels. Lucifer lost the battle and was cast out of Heaven, with his followers, down to Earth. *"Jesus replied: 'I saw Satan fall like lightning from heaven'"* – Luke 10:18 NIV.

Satan wasn't finished yet! He took the form of a snake in the Garden of Eden to tempt Eve. He convinced Eve that God was keeping something good from her by not allowing her to eat from the tree of the knowledge of good and evil. *"You will not surely die,' the serpent said to the woman. 'For God knows that when you eat of it your eyes will be opened, and you will be like God, knowing good and evil.'"* – Genesis 3:4-5 NIV. Then he used Eve to tempt Adam into sin. So Satan, the fall, death, all came from a desire to be like God instead of being a servant of God.

> Men occasionally stumble over the truth, but most of them pick themselves up and hurry off as if nothing had happened. – Winston Churchill

Satan wants to deceive everyone just like he did to Eve in the garden. He is the father of deception. He uses his beauty and wisdom to deceive nations and people. *"For false Christs and false prophets will appear and perform great signs and miracles to deceive even the elect – if that were possible."* – Matthew 24:24 NIV. *"Watch out for false prophets. They come to you in sheep's clothing, but inwardly they are ferocious wolves."* – Matthew 7:15 NIV.

Many Christians believe that Satan is this guy in a red devil suit, or looks like a cartoon devil. That's not who he is. He is a beautiful and wise angel that has rebelled. No wonder people question the history of Satan since people don't believe or are skeptical whether he exists or not. Satan has been free to influence them without being discovered as the cause of their problems. *"Be very careful, then, how you live – not as unwise but as wise, making the most of every opportunity, because the days are evil. Therefore do not be foolish, but understand what the Lord's will is." – Ephesians 5:15-17 NIV.*

Satan wants to do nothing more than take away the joy and good relationship of Christians through deception and temptation.

Yes Satan is powerful. However, with Jesus Christ on our side we need not fear Satan's limited power but we ought to be wise in resisting his tactics. *"For though we live in the world, we do not wage war as the world does. The weapons we fight with are not the weapons of the world. On the contrary, they have divine power to demolish strongholds. We demolish arguments and every pretension that sets itself up against the knowledge of God, and we take captive every thought to make it obedient to Christ. And we will be ready to punish every act of disobedience, once your obedience is complete." – 2 Corinthians 10:3-6 NIV.*

> *But the Lord is faithful, and he will strengthen and protect you from the evil one. – 2 Thessalonians 3:3 NIV*

"Because God's children are human beings – made of flesh and blood by being born in human form. For only as a human being could He die, and only by dying could He break the power of the devil, who had the power of death. [15] Only in this way could He deliver those who have lived all their lives as slaves to the fear of dying." – Hebrews 2:14-15 NIV.

Notice at the end of the first verse it says "had." Satan had the power of death by convincing Adam and Eve to sin and bring it upon them. Satan has no power to kill unless allowed by God (Job 2:4-6). Also in the second verse God delivered Christians from the fear of dying. We no longer have to be afraid of death, because to die in Christ is gain.

Throughout history Satan's evil has been identified because he is directly opposite of God's character. God's purpose is to lead people to salvation while the devil's is to lead people into rebellion. God tells the truth but the devil lies. God's motivation is love while Satan's is hate. When you follow Christ you experience love, peace, joy, kindness, etc. Satan's followers experience sexual immorality, impurity, idolatry, hatred, jealousy, envy, rage, which all lead to death.

When you follow Christ you are freed from sin, when you follow Satan you become enslaved to sin.

Many people (even some Christians) are being overpowered by Satan. Why? Because we have developed errors in our beliefs. One error is denying that Satan even exists. Another is fearfully focusing on Satan rather than on Christ Jesus who overcame him. Another is the people outright worshiping Satan, preferring the darkness of evil rather than the light that reveals sin. All of these "errors" please Satan. He wants us denying, fearing, obeying, and worshiping him. We must not let that happen! We must focus on the one true God, the One who loves us, and protects us!

In conclusion, the devil brings confusion and chaos, while God brings a love that's simply unconditional and satisfying.

The devil is crafty; he always promises something but can never really live up to that promise. Sin, the devil, evil, they don't satisfy – they just deceive; they mess with your brain. God's love is truly satisfying.

Question

1. Is the devil ever upfront and clear?

Twenty-seven

Common Questions

Many of us have questions and/or statements about God that we either want to know or have been asked; so I'm going to take some time to address a few popular statements and questions.

Statement 1: "Seeing is believing; if I can't see it I don't believe it exists."

Answer: We believe in many things that we cannot see. Have you ever seen air? Have you seen history? Have you ever seen your brain, heart or lungs? We see effects of air. We have records of history, but it is by "faith" we believe that certain historical events happened. Wi-Fi is invisible, but your phone can detect the presence of the internet. Man has a "Wi-Fi receiver" in his soul; however, the receiver is broken because of sin. *"And you hath he quickened, who were dead in trespasses and sins." – Ephesians 2:1 KJV.* You need to be plugged into the life of God. Then you will be aware of the invisible spiritual realm, and be spiritually electrified. Have God reset your router.

Statement 2: "I don't feel guilty, that means I never committed a sin."

Answer: People often don't feel guilty when they sin because they have "severed" their conscience. They have removed the batteries from the smoke alarm of their conscience, so that they can sin without interruption.

Statement 3: "I know that I am a sinner, but I confess my sins to God each night. I tell him that I am sorry and that I won't sin again."

Answer: If you are in court with a $100,000 fine, will the judge let you go simply because you say that you are sorry and that you won't commit the crime again? Of course not! You should be sorry for breaking the law, and shouldn't commit the crime again; but, if someone stepped in and paid the $100,000 fine, then you would be free to go. God will not forgive a sinner simply because he said "sorry." Of course we should be sorry for sin. We have a conscience to tell us that rape, murder, hatred, lying, and stealing, etc., are wrong, and we shouldn't sin again. God will, however, release us from the demands of eternal justice on the basis that someone else paid our fine. Two thousand years ago Jesus Christ paid the price in full for the sins of the world. His words on the cross were, "It is finished." In other words, the debt has been paid in full. All who repent (which means turning away from your sins) and trust in Him receive remission of sins. Their case is dismissed on the basis of His blood and death.

Statement 4: When you are dead, you are dead. There's no afterlife.

Answer: What if you are wrong? What if God, Jesus, the prophets, the Christians, are right and you are wrong? You would be in some deep trouble if the Christians are right and you are wrong!

If there is no after life, no judgment day, no Heaven or Hell, then God is unjust and each of the above are guilty of being false witnesses. It means that Almighty God couldn't care less about the fact that a man rapes a woman, then cuts her throat and is never brought to justice. If you are right, and there is no ultimate justice, you won't even have the joy of saying "I told you so." However, if you are wrong you will lose your soul and end up eternally damned. You are playing Russian roulette with a fully loaded gun.

Statement 5: "God sure blew it, Creation is a mess!

Answer: There are three million people who die from mosquito bites each year. Hurricanes, tornadoes, floods, and other disasters slaughter tens of thousands. We have devastating droughts; multitudes crippled with arthritis, children dying of leukemia, masses of other cancerous diseases, endless suffering, unspeakable pain and death. What sort of "tyrant" would create us and then give us all this grief? Especially if God is an "all-loving" Father figure, as we are often told that He is. We seem to have three choices. One: God blew it when he made everything (He's creative but incompetent). Two: God is a tyrant, who gets His kicks from seeing kids die of leukemia. Three: Something between God and man is radically wrong. There's our choice! <u>Something between man and God is radically wrong.</u> The Bible tells us what it is. There is a war going on. We are told that mankind is an enemy of God in his mind through wicked works. That's not too hard to see. We are forever committing murder, rape, lying, and stealing. WE USE GOD'S NAME AS A CURSE WORD while "Mother Nature" gets the glory for His creation. (Unless there's a horrible disaster. Then man calls that "an act of God.")

An applicable acronym for "war" is "We Are Right." That's why any country goes to war, because it believes that it is right. A couple moments of going through God's law shows us who is right and who is wrong. We, not God, are the guilty party. If we want His blessing back on our nation, we must make peace with Him, and that can only happen through faith in Jesus Christ.

Statement 6: "When I was younger I used to lie and steal but that was years ago."

Answer: Time does not forgive sins. If someone commits murder on Saturday, then goes to church on Sunday, he is still a murderer. If someone lies and steals, unless he comes to the Savior, his sins remain with him until he stands before God in judgment.

Statement 7: "I've tried reading the Bible, but I can't understand it."

Answer: I would suggest you check your version of the Bible. If you are a new Christian I would suggest you don't start right off with the King James Version, I would start with the New King James or The New International Version. You should always start your Bible study with prayer; ask God what He wants to show you in a certain passage. Also when reading the Bible, expect it to change you. If you read the Bible thinking that nothing will happen, then nothing will happen. You must read it with the intention of being changed by it.

Statement 8: "Christians are just a bunch of haters."

Answer: A lot of unbelievers think that our warning about God's judgment and Hell shows hatred towards them. But it's quite the opposite! We love them so much that we don't want them to face Jesus Christ and be cast into Hell; so we warn them. We love them so much that we want them in Heaven with us. If we hated the unbelievers, we would either refuse to give them the gospel, or lie and pretend they are saved by making them comfortable as they head for Hell. Jesus shed His blood to wash away our sins and He rose from the dead three days later. That is anything but hatred! That is what Christians are trying to tell the unsaved. It is Jesus' love message for everyone; not a hate message.

Question 1: Didn't just mere men write the Bible?

Answer: Yes. When you write a letter, do you write the letter, or does the pen? Obviously you do; the pen is merely the instrument you use. God used men as instruments to write His "letter," "His-story" to humanity. The writers ranged from kings to common fishermen, but the 66 books of the Bible were all given by the inspiration of God. Proof that this book is supernatural can be seen with a quick study of its many prophecies.

Questions 2: Are Christians better than non-Christians?

Answer: A Christian is no better than a non-Christian; he is

Jacob E. Wilcox

however better off. It is like two men in a boat out at sea. One is wearing a life jacket and the other isn't. One is not better than the other, but the man with a life jacket on is certainly better off. The difference will be seen when the boat springs a leak and sinks out in the deep sea. Jesus warned that if we go into death without Him, we would perish. It is a fearful thing to fall into the hands of God as a sinner.

Question 3: Will the people who never heard the gospel go to Hell?

Answer: No one will go to Hell because they haven't heard of Jesus Christ. The sinner will go to Hell for murder, rape, adultery, lust, etc., sin is not failing to hear the Gospel; sin is transgression of the law. If we really care about them, we will become missionaries and take the good news of God's forgiveness in Christ to them. *"Whosoever committeth sin transgresseth also the law: for sin is the transgression of the law." – 1 John 3:4 KJV.*

Question 4: Don't Christians sin too?

Answer: If a Christian sins, he falls rather than dives into sin. He resists rather than embraces it. Any dead fish can float down stream. It takes a live one to swim against the flow. What we must do is get right back up and keep fighting even harder.

> *If ye then be risen with Christ, seek those things which are above, where Christ sitteth on the right hand of God. Set your affection on things above, not on things on the earth. – Colossians 3:1-2 KJV*

Question 5: Is gluttony a sin?

Answer: *Whether therefore ye eat, or drink, or whatsoever ye do, do all to the glory of God. – 1 Corinthians 10:31 KJV.* Gluttony is a sin that Christians seem to ignore. Eating too much has nothing to do with being fat because a skinny person could be a glutton also, but obesity could be a result of the continuing sin of gluttony.

We are often quick to say drinking and smoking are sins, but for some reason gluttony is accepted or if anything, tolerated. The argument used against smoking and drinking, such as health and addiction, apply equally to overeating. *"Every man is tempted, when he is drawn away of his own lust, and enticed." – James 1:14 KJV.*

Many Christians wouldn't even consider having a glass of wine or a cigarette but don't care if they gorge themselves at the dinner table.

Gluttony is a sin and one that should be discussed more in churches. Overeating is idolatry and it is very dangerous. Overeating is very harmful and addicting. That is why in the Bible it is compared to drunkenness and laziness. *"Do not join those who drink too much wine or gorge themselves on meat, for drunkards and gluttons become poor, and drowsiness clothes them in rags." – Proverbs 23:20-21 NIV.*

Our appetite is an analogy of our ability to control ourselves. If we can't control our eating habits, we probably won't be able to control other habits like lust, greed, hatred, etc. We are to have control over our eating habits. *"If you find honey, eat just enough too much of it, and you will vomit." – Proverbs 25:26 NIV. "It is not good to eat too much honey, nor is it honorable to seek one's own honor." – Proverbs 25:27 NIV.*

> *Don't you know that you yourselves are God's temple and that God's Spirit lives in you? If anyone destroys God's temple, God will destroy him; for God's temple is sacred, and you are that temple. – 1 Corinthians 3:16-17 NIV*

God has blessed us by filling this world with great tasting, nutritious foods. We should respect God's creation by eating appropriate quantities of these foods. Don't let your appetite control you.

And yes, there is so much temptation to overeat. We have pizza, chicken, restaurants, all-you-can-eat buffets, but Christians are to control our appetite and keep our body healthy. *"I discipline my body like an athlete, training it to do what it should. Otherwise, I fear that after preaching to others I myself might be disqualified." – 1 Corinthians 9:27 NLT.*

One reason that gluttony is so "popular" is that it's brought on by boredom. "There's nothing to do, I'll just sit down and watch some TV and eat this food." Find something better to do with your time. Invest your time exercising or reading God's Word.

Resist the devil when he tempts you with cravings when you're not even hungry. Pray to God for help to overcome this sin.

Question 6: Where is the evidence for God's existence?

Answer: Many people deny a Creator all together because of lack of evidence. Those people don't look deep enough or hard enough to uncover anything, or they look too deep and over-complicate it.

For this answer I will name a few evidences of a Divine Creator. Let's start with our bodies. The human brain processes an amazing amount of information. Your brain takes in all the colors and objects you see, the temperature around you, the sounds around you, even the texture of the book that you are holding. The human brain processes more than a million messages a second.

The brain functions differently than other organs. There is intelligence to it, the ability to reason, to produce feelings, to take action, and to relate.

The brain simply couldn't have evolved from billions of years. It has the fingerprint of God on it.

What about the eye? The eye can distinguish many different colors; it also has an automatic focusing system. There is so much detail in the human eye, that evolution simply cannot fully explain the initial source of it. Our bodies are so complex and unique; there is just no way we could have come about by mere chance!

What about the universe? Life might seem uncertain, but look at what is certain: gravity remains consistent, the days are 24 hours, and speed of light doesn't change, on Earth or in galaxies far away.

Why is it that the laws of nature never change? Why is the universe so orderly and reliable? The greatest scientists have been struck by how strange this is. There is no logical necessity for a universe that obeys rules, let alone one that abides by the rules of mathematics. This astonishment comes from the recognition that the universe doesn't have to behave this way.

Now what about Earth? The Earth is the perfect size. It is the only known planet equipped with an atmosphere of the right mixture of gasses to sustain life. The Earth is at the perfect distance from the sun. If it were any further away we would freeze, if it was the slightest bit closer the sun would make it impossible for life to be here. The Earth is also rotating on an axis, allowing the entire surface of the Earth to be properly warmed and cooled every day.

Our moon is the perfect size and distance from the Earth for its gravitational pull. The moon creates important ocean tides and movement so ocean waters do not stagnate, and yet our massive oceans are restrained from spilling over across the continents.

What about the most important life giving chemical? H_2O, or water. Water is odorless, colorless and without taste, yet no living thing can survive without it. The human body is about two-thirds water. Water allows us to live in an environment of fluctuating temperature changes, while keeping our bodies a steady 98.6 degrees.

Water has a unique surface tension. Water in plants can flow upward against gravity because of this surface tension, bringing life-giving water and nutrients to the top of even the tallest tree.

Ninety-seven percent of the Earth's water is in the oceans. But there is a system which removes salt from the water and then distributes that water throughout the globe. Evaporation takes the ocean waters, leaving the salt, and forms clouds which are easily moved by the wind to disperse water over the land, for vegetation, animals, and people. Now isn't that just a coincidence! Water freezes from the top down and floats, so that fish can live in the winter.

Look at the "paths" in the ocean. How is it that the water is not dispersing once it hits the ocean? Take a garden hose and put it in a large pool or small lake. What happens? The water comes out a little ways then disperses into the pool water leaving no trace. The Gulf Stream is a "river" in the ocean that goes by Florida then up to England. It's a literal river that goes through the ocean. How is that possible?

It takes an intelligent Creator to make a complicated design.

There is <u>so</u> much evidence that God exists. You cannot deny it; it's a fact.

Now I challenge you, if you or a friend doesn't believe in an all powerful Creator, to give legitimate proof of how there is <u>NO</u> Creator.

Twenty-eight

The Salvation Message

*The Lord is my light and my Salvation; whom
shall I fear? The Lord is the strength of my life; of
whom shall I be afraid? – Psalms 27:1 KJV*

*Restore unto me the joy of thy Salvation; and uphold
me with thy free spirit. – Psalms 51:12 KJV*

*Behold, God is my Salvation; I will trust, and not
be afraid: for the Lord Jehovah is my strength and
my song; he also is become my Salvation.
– Isaiah 12:2 KJV.*

*For therefore we both labor and suffer reproach, because
we trust in the living God, who is the savior of all men,
specially of those that believe. – 1 Timothy 4:10 KJV*

*If your sinful nature controls your mind, there is death. But if the
Holy Spirit controls your mind, there is life and peace. For the sinful
nature is always hostile to God. It never did obey God's laws, and
it never will. That's why those who are still under the control of
their sinful nature can never please God. But you are not controlled
by your sinful nature. You are controlled by the Spirit if you have
the Spirit of God living in you. (And remember that those who
do not have the Spirit of Christ living in them are not Christians
at all.) Since Christ lives within you, even though your body will*

Jacob E. Wilcox

die because of sin, the Spirit will bring you eternal life because
you have been made right with God. – Romans 8:6-10 NLT

"We are to mourn for our spiritual state, to surrender
our prideful heart, and then we can find peace in Christ Jesus."
– Steve Queen.

What is Salvation? Salvation is "the act of saving; preservation
from destruction, danger or great calamity; appropriately in theology,
the redemption of man from the bondage of
sin and liability to eternal death, and the
confessing on him everlasting happiness." So
what's God's Salvation? God says in His
Word that He sent His Son to save us from
all our sins. God sent His Son to die on the cross for you! HE DIED
FOR YOU! So if you're thinking that you're not special, just
remember that you are so important to God that He decided to die
for you. You must be a pretty important person for someone to die
for you. Just think how many people around you would even consider
taking a bullet for you. It's very rare for someone to die for someone
else. *"Greater love hath no one man than this that a man lay down his*
life for his friends." – John 15:13 KJV.

> *Jesus' crucifixion gives us salvation from our sins!*

So this Jesus guy died for me, but why? Jesus loved us so much
That He laid down His life so that we could find peace. Believe it or
not you are God's child, you are a child of God, you were made in
his image and He loves you beyond measure; but just like all ignorant
children we disobey we were born
with a spark of rebellion in us.

> It's not too late God loves you even when you sin. He is more than willing to forgive and welcome you into His kingdom.

When Adam and Eve sinned in
the garden, they were separated
from the direct presence with our
Father; and as a result of their
disobedience the curse echoed

throughout history and is in effect today. We were on a collision course with death and Hell. There was no way to lead us back into the path of righteousness. So God sent His Son to go into the world to die so that we could have direct contact with our Creator, and allow His blood to wipe away our sins. But when He died it wasn't over. In three days He rose from the dead. HE CONQUERED DEATH!!!! Death couldn't hold God's Son from Him. God raised Jesus from the dead so that He could be an advocate for Him. If

> *Examine yourselves to see whether you are in the faith; test yourselves. Do you not realize that Christ Jesus is in you unless, of course, you fail the test? – 2 Corinthians 13:5 NIV*

God hadn't sent His Son we would still be sacrificing our best animal to barely cover our sins. You see, Jesus was the ultimate sacrifice for every sin we have committed. His blood didn't just cover our sins, it wiped them away permanently. Now if we sin we can go directly to our Father to ask for forgiveness. The blood has already been spilled at the cross.

We were all on the pathway to Hell but God provided a different direction. We just need to follow where He is leading us. Jesus said in John 14:6 – "I am the way, the truth, and the life: no man cometh unto the father, but by me." So follow Jesus! Yes, it will get hard, the devil will be on you like white on rice. You just need the courage and faith that comes from God to make it through the troublesome times. If you are not saved then I encourage you to ask Jesus to save you. Nobody else can save your soul; only Jesus can. Give your heart to Jesus. "...If thou shalt confess with thy mouth the Lord Jesus, and shalt believe in thine heart that God hath raised Him from the dead, thou shalt be saved." – Romans 10:9 KJV.

"For I resolved to know nothing while I was with you except Jesus Christ and Him crucified." – 1 Corinthians 2:2 NIV. We need to decide on important issues in life. We can't stay on the fence – we need to be on one side or the other.

Here are three things that you need to resolve in your life: your salvation, your purity, and your faith.

Here are four things you need to do to give your heart to Jesus:

1) Admit that you are a sinner. *"As it is written there is none righteous, no, not one." – Romans 3:10 KJV.*

2) 2) Be willing to turn from your sins; repent. *"And the times of this ignorance God winked at; but now commandeth all men everywhere to repent." – Acts 17:30 KJV.*

> Christians seem to have lost their focus on Jesus' core message: 'Love the Lord your God with all your heart and with all your soul, and love your neighbor as you love yourself.' – R.M. Tacoma

3) 3) Believe that Jesus Christ died for you, was buried, and rose from the dead. *"If thou confess with thy mouth the Lord Jesus, and shalt believe in thine heart that God hath raised him from the dead, thou shalt be saved. For with the heart man believeth unto righteousness; and with the mouth confession is made unto Salvation." – Romans 10:9-10 KJV.*

4) 4) And finally through prayer, invite Jesus into your life to become your personal Savior. *"For whosoever shall call upon the name of the Lord shall be saved." – Romans 10:13 KJV.*

If you don't know what to pray then just say this prayer: "Dear God, I am a sinner and in need of forgiveness. I believe that Jesus Christ shed His precious blood and died for my sins. I am willing to turn away from my sinful life. I ask that You will forgive my sins that I have committed. I now invite You to come into my heart and life as my personal Savior." If you have said that prayer honestly and trust in Jesus as your Lord and Savior, then you have just begun a wonderful new life with Him! Now you must read your Bible to get to know Jesus and His Words better.

Talk with a pastor or Christian friend and ask them to be an accountability partner to you. Talk to God in prayer every day. And most importantly talk to others about Jesus Christ. Spread the word about how He saved you. If you have done what this chapter says, then you are truly now electrified.

Defensive Action Against Sin

Anyone who hides his sins doesn't succeed. But anyone who admits His sins and gives them up finds mercy. – Proverbs 28:13 NIV

"Satan wants to allure us into acting as our own god, sourcing ourselves; to not be totally dependent upon the spirit of Jesus."
– Steve Queen 2016

Now that you have allowed God into your life, you must now seek to keep the sin that filled that void out. Every sin you commit is seen by God. Even the most secretive ones are seen by Him; He sees everything we do. It's hard hiding sins from Him, so don't hide your sins, confess them to God and ask for forgiveness and He is "faithful and just to forgive."

Like I said earlier, "keep your mind sharp," because you never know when the devil will attack you. He will pounce on you with everything he has, so have strength – mentally and spiritually. The best thing you could do for defense is to avoid the fight. If you feel that Satan's going to strike at an area in your life, then flee!

> If you allow enough mess in your life it will kill you.

Don't walk into the trap; run from it before it entangles you. If you do find yourself in the trap, take up your weapon of choice: God! Keep God close to you so that He can protect you. He can't protect you in a battle when you're 100 feet away from Him trying to fight the battle yourself! So get close to Him.

The devil knows when and where you are most vulnerable, so

strengthen the defenses in those places in your life that are weak. Strengthen your defenses in all areas of your life. Don't just focus on one sin in your life. This is an example of an unbalanced defensive wall: You could be winning a battle of lust over on one side of your wall, but on the other side your wall has been breached because you are excelling in lying and hatred. A good thing to do is just give your hardships and stuff you're struggling with to God.

Another defensive weapon that's essential for stopping any kind of temptation and sin is: memorizing key scripture. It will help you "modernize" your defensive wall. Invest your time into memorizing scripture. To help you find the right scripture I have included some scriptures at the end of this book for memorizing purposes. When you invest your time into reading and studying the Word of God, you will be rewarded with a strong wall of defense. We all have twenty-four hours in a day. If we spend only one hour of studying and talking to God, and the rest of the time we're just doing what we want to do, then we won't build the strong wall we desire. Spend as much time with God as possible. He is your best friend. Treat Him like one.

Ministering And Serving

Like I said at the beginning of this book, if you want to minister to teenagers you need to not be pushy. Being pushy will only lead to them leaving the church altogether. Trust me when I say being pushy is bad but understand too that there's a difference between being pushy and being determined. Being pushy is trying to make them come to church every time the doors open. Being determined is to <u>invite </u>them to church or events that your church hosts every once in awhile.

Conclusion

One of the main essences of being a Christian is forgiveness; forgiveness is what makes us different from the world. Forgiveness is the most important thing to do for someone. If we don't forgive others then God won't forgive us. And yes, it is hard to forgive someone, they might have done the worst thing possible to you or your family, but you need to still forgive them.

> Don't support evil; don't get caught up in the worldly life. We are here temporarily.

The world is unforgiving, but we are not supposed to act like the world – we are to remain separate from this sinful world. We are to be transformed by Jesus not conformed to this world. We are different, so act like it! The one thing Jesus hates is "pretenders," which are people who say they are Christian but their actions speak otherwise. For instance, a Christian says he's against alcohol yet he drinks wine every so often.

Another thing that you need to do as teenage Christians is: Don't cross any of your Godly standards just to keep a friend or boy/girl friend (like I said earlier). Keep your spiritual walls up. The direction your life will take is influenced by what kind of people you let into your life, and mind. Keep your mind sharp. Make sure that you have firm control over your mind. Your mind is like a sponge; it absorbs everything. You need a filter to separate the bad from good. God is that filter. Think before you speak; think to yourself, is what I'm about to say pleasing to God? If not, then don't say it.

> God will give us victory only if we lean on Him. – Steve Queen. 2016

Another thing you need to know that I've already touched on is: just because you are a good person doesn't mean you will go to Heaven. You must ask Jesus into your heart and live according to His Word if you want to be saved. Good people don't go to Heaven; it's the saved people that do.

"But I am afraid that, as the serpent deceived Eve by his craftiness, your minds will be led astray from the simplicity and purity of devotion to Christ. – 2 Corinthians 11:3 NASB. God's salvation message is so simple just like this verse says. Sometimes its simplicity confuses people.

> Wise men talk because they have something to say, but fools talk because they have to say something. – Plato

Being a Christian isn't checking off your spiritual check list. It's about knowing God and having a spiritual connection with Him. Many a time Christians make God's salvation complicated by telling you what you have to do and how to act. But, it's simple: obey God and do what <u>HE</u> tells you to do out of love.

Live the life that HE wishes for you; not what others put on you.

Embrace the spiritual electricity that the Father gives you.

Live a radical Christian life and you will have a radical Holy response from God.

Live to please God, not people.

Live to inspire others to become radically electrified.

Become who God wants you to be.

A life without God is death; but a life with Him will electrify you beyond measure.

So go teens and young adults! Go and be seed planters for God's kingdom. Plant seeds of righteousness in others. Go start the spark; light the match; flip the switch, so that you and your companions can be truly electrified in Christ.

Sincerely: Jacob E. Wilcox

Scripture

What I've gathered from life is that you need to know God's Word to be able to stand against the enemy. When the devil tries to tempt you, or discourage you, you can recite some scripture that can relate to what the devil's trying to convince you of. So here are some great scriptures that I have come across and used in my studies. I hope God's Word will help, may it be a lamp unto your feet and a light for your path.

> *You received Christ Jesus as Lord. So keep on living*
> *in him. Have your roots in him. Build yourselves up*
> *in him. Grow strong in what you believe, just as you*
> *were taught. Be more thankful than ever before.*
> *– Colossians 2:6-7 NIV*

> *I will say of the Lord, "He is my refuge and my fortress,*
> *my God, in whom I trust." – Psalms 91:2 NIV*

> *But the Lord watches over those who fear him, those who rely*
> *on his unfailing love. He rescues them from death and keeps*
> *them alive in times of famine. – Psalms 33:18-19 NLT*

> *Whom have I in heaven but thee? And there is none upon earth that*
> *I desire besides thee. My flesh and my heart faileth: but God is the*
> *strength of my heart, and my portion forever. – Psalms 73:25-26 KJV*

> *The Lord is my shepherd, I shall not be in want. He makes me*
> *lie down in green pastures, he leads me beside quiet waters, he*
> *restores my soul. He guides me in the paths of righteousness for*

his name's sake. Even though I walk through the valley of the shadow of death, I will fear no evil, for you are with me; your rod and your staff, they comfort me. You prepare a table before me in the presence of my enemies. You anoint my head with oil; my cup overflows. Surly goodness and love will follow me all the days of my life, and I will dwell in the house of the Lord forever.
– Psalms 23 NIV

Praise ye the Lord: For it is good to sing praises unto our God; for it is pleasant; and praise is comely. – Psalms 147:1 KJV

He healeth the broken in heart, and bindeth up their wounds. – Psalms 147:3 KJV.

Turn your worries over to the Lord. He will keep you going. He will never let godly people fall. – Psalms 55:22 NIV

The Lord is my light and my salvation; whom shall I fear? The Lord is the strength of my life; of whom shall I be afraid? – Psalms 27:1 KJV

The thief comes only to steal and kill and destroy; I have come that they may have life, and have it to the full. – John 10:10 NIV

If we confess our sins, he is faithful and just and will forgive us our sins and purify us from all unrighteousness. – 1 John 1:9 NIV

Do not withhold good from those who deserve it, when it is in your power to act. – Proverbs 3:27 NIV

The Lord is far from the wicked but hears the prayer of the righteous. – Proverbs 15:29 NIV

He who conceals his sins does not prosper, but whoever confesses and renounces them finds mercy. – Proverbs 28:13 NIV

Enter not into the path of the wicked, and go not in the way of evil men. – Proverbs 4:14 KJV

When you lie down, you will not be afraid; when you lie down, your sleep will be sweet. – Proverbs 3:24 NIV

The heart of the righteous studieth to answer: But the mouth of the wicked poureth out evil things. – Proverbs 15:28 KJV

He who walks with the wise grows wise, but a companion of fools suffers harm. – Proverbs 13:20 NIV

The godly give good advice to their friends; the wicked lead them astray. – Proverbs 12:26 NLT

The fear of the Lord is the beginning of knowledge, but fools despise wisdom and discipline. – Proverbs 1:7 NIV

The wicked man flees though no one pursues, but the righteous are as bold as a lion. – Proverbs 28:1 NIV

…If anyone would come after me, he must deny himself and take up his cross daily and follow me. For whoever wants to save his life will lose it, but whoever loses his life for me will save it. What good is it for a man to gain the whole world, and yet lose or forfeit his very self? – Luke 9:23-25 NIV

If anyone is ashamed of me and my words, the Son of Man will be ashamed of him when he comes in his glory and in the glory of the Father and of the holy angels. – Luke 9:26 NIV

Do not be misled: bad company corrupts good character. – 1 Corinthians 15:33 NIV

I know very well how foolish the message of the cross sounds to those who are on the road to destruction. But we who are being saved recognize this message as the very power of God.
— 1 Corinthians 1:18 NLT

But God commandeth his love toward us, in that, while we were yet sinners, Christ died for us. — Romans 5:8 KJV

For the wages of sin is death; but the gift of God is eternal life through Jesus Christ our Lord. — Romans 6:23 KJV

If we live, we live to honor the Lord. If we die, we die to honor the Lord. So whether we live or die, we belong to the Lord.
— Romans 14:8 NIV

Without faith it is impossible to please God, because anyone who comes to Him must believe that he exits. And that he rewards those who earnestly seek Him. — Hebrews 11:6 NIV

But those who hope in the Lord will renew their strength. They will soar on wings like eagles; they will run and not grow weary, they will walk and not be faint. — Isaiah 40:31 NIV

Fear thou not; for I am with thee: Be not dismayed; for I am thy God: I will strengthen thee; Yea, I will help thee; Yea, I will uphold thee with the right hand of my righteousness. — Isaiah 41:10 KJV

"For I know the plans I have for you," declares the Lord, "plans to prosper you and not to harm you, plans to give you hope and a future."
— Jeremiah 29:11 NIV

The Lord is not slow in keeping His promises, as some understand slowness. He is patient with you, not wanting anyone to perish, but everyone to come to repentance. — 2 Peter 3:9 NIV

Flee the evil desires of youth, and pursue righteousness, faith, love and peace, along with those who call on the Lord out of a pure heart.
– 2 Timothy 2:22 NIV

Don't have anything to do with foolish and stupid arguments, because you know they produce quarrels. And the Lords servant must not quarrel; instead, he must be kind to everyone, able to teach, not resentful.
– 2 Timothy 2:23-24 NIV

... Everyone who wants to live a godly life in Christ Jesus will be persecuted. – 2 Timothy 3:12 NIV

For God hath not given us the spirit of fear; but of power, and of love, and of a sound mind. – 2 Timothy 1:7 KJV

Be completely humble and gentle; be patient, bearing with one another in love. Make every effort to keep the unity of the Spirit through the bond of peace. – Ephesians 4:2-3 NIV

Do not be deceived: God cannot be mocked. A man reaps what he sows. The one who sows to please his sinful nature, from that nature will reap destruction; the one who sows to please the Spirit, from the Spirit will reap eternal life. – Galatians 6:7 NIV

Before I formed you in the womb I knew you, before you were born I set you apart; I appointed you as a prophet to the nations.
– Jeremiah 1:5 NIV

Acknowledgements

Special thanks to everyone who has sponsored me and given me ideas, information, and/or encouragement while I was writing this book. I am truly very thankful to all of you.

Honorable Mentions:

Our Lord Jesus Christ
My Family and Friends in faith
Creation Crusaders Ministry
Debra Hill
Erika Danver
Stephanie Grimes
Todd Barlow
Pastor Steve Queen
Pastor Wayne Searls

Glossary

Addiction: The fact or condition of being addicted to a particular substance, thing, or activity.

Adultery: Voluntary sexual intercourse between a married person and a person who is not his or her spouse.

Advocate: A person who publicly supports or recommends a particular cause or policy.

Boundary: A line that marks the limits of an area; a dividing line.

Bully: Someone who uses superior strength or influence to intimidate someone, typically to force him or her to do what one wants.

Cherub: A winged angelic being described in biblical tradition as attending on God. It is represented in ancient Middle Eastern art as a lion or bull with eagle's wings and a human face, and regarded in traditional Christian angelology as an angel of the second highest order of the nine-fold celestial hierarchy.

Condescending: Having or showing a feeling of patronizing superiority.

Conform: Behave according to socially acceptable conventions or standards.

Covenant: An agreement that brings about a relationship of commitment between God and His people.

Evolution: The process by which different kinds of living organisms are thought to have developed and diversified from earlier forms during the history of the Earth.

Gap Theory: A form of old Earth creationism.

Gluttony: Excessive eating disorder.

Heaven: A place regarded as the abode of God and the angels and of the good after death.

Hell: A place regarded as a spiritual realm of evil and suffering, often traditionally depicted as a place of perpetual fire beneath the Earth where the wicked are punished after death.

Idolatry: The worship of idols. Extreme admiration, love, or reverence for something or someone.

Intoxication: The state of being intoxicated, especially by alcohol.

Judeo-Christian: Judeo-Christian groups Judaism and Christianity, either in reference to their common origin in Late Antiquity or due to perceived parallels or commonalities shared between the two traditions.

Lust: Very strong sexual desire for someone.

Manhood: The state or period of being a man rather than a child. The process of growing into "manhood" qualities traditionally associated with men, such as courage, and strength.

Marriage: The legally or formally recognized union of a man and a woman as partners in a relationship.

Monogamous, Monogamy: Being married to, or in a sexual relationship with, one person at a time. Humans are one of the few species that practice monogamy. (Well, sometimes. You may have heard of something called polygamy, which is having more than one spouse at a time.)

Morals: A person's standard of behavior or beliefs concerning what is and is not acceptable for them to do.

Pornography: Printed or visual material containing the explicit description or display of sexual actions.

Pre-biotic: Existing or occurring before the emergence of life.

Progressive creationism: The belief that God created new forms of life gradually over a period of hundreds of millions of years.

Prophecy: A prediction of future events.

Radical: Relating to or affecting the fundamental nature of something; far-reaching or thorough.

Relapse: Suffer deterioration after a period of improvement.

Sin: An immoral act considered to be a transgression against divine law.

Sinner: A person who transgresses against divine law by committing an immoral act or acts.

Spoiler: A person or thing that spoils something by disclosing the outcome of an event or story before the ending.

Transcendent: Beyond or above the range of normal or merely physical human experience; surpassing the ordinary.

Transform: To make a dramatic change in appearance or character.

Trivialize: To make something seem less important, significant, or complex than it really is.

Values: The regard that something is held to deserve; the importance, worth, or usefulness of something; a person's principles or standards of behavior; one's judgment of what is important in life.

Works Cited

Arterburn, Stephen and Fred Stoeker. (2004). *Every Young Man's Battle.* Waterbrook.

Chick, Jack T. Chick Publications.

Landis, Don (2014). *The Genius of Ancient Man.* Master Books.

Morris, Dr. Harry (2012). *The Henry Morris KJV Study Bible.* Master Books.

Padgett, Anthony (2003). *Journey to Agape.* From the Ashes Publishing.

Strachan, Owen. "Wishing Away God's Design".

Webster's Pocket Dictionary

King James Bible

New American Standard Bible

New International Version

New King James Bible

New Living Translation

Printed in the United States
By Bookmasters